T0293936

THE THIRTIES AND THE NINETIES

JULIAN SYMONS

The Thirties
and the Nineties

CARCANET

This edition first published in Great Britain in 1990 by
Carcanet Press Limited
208-212 Corn Exchange Buildings
Manchester M4 3BQ

British Library Cataloguing in Publication Data

Symons, Julian, *1912-*
    The thirties and the nineties.
    1. Great Britain. Intellectual life
    I. Title
    941.081

    ISBN 0-85635-902-5

The publisher acknowledges financial assistance
from the Arts Council of Great Britain

Set in 10pt Baskerville by Bryan Williamson, Darwen
Printed and bound in England by SRP Ltd, Exeter

FOR MARCUS SYMONS

in 1960

The circle narrows as the child grows taller.
The mirage vanishes as we go nearer.
Though when we're older we may see things clearer
The colour's duller and the shapes are smaller.

For you whose thoughts are still a daze of heroes
This will appear a tale of half-men, zeroes.
Freed from our hopes and monsters, dreams and terrors,
Look tolerantly upon these lives and errors.

Contents

THE THIRTIES
A DREAM REVOLVED

1
The Background

I was looking again into *Texts and Pretexts* when it occurred to me that the form used by Aldous Huxley for this book, a blend of quotation and discursive comment, might be adapted in writing about the 1930s. The idea of making a book about the Thirties had been in my mind for a long while: some sort of anthology, The Best of Thirties Verse, perhaps – it was in these hackneyed terms that my thoughts moved first. But the best Thirties verse is pretty well known, and the feeling of a decade isn't caught by displaying little gems of poetry, however genuine and typical. And may not bad verse be as typical as good? For a reader distant in time from the Thirties to understand much about them such a book would have to include not only good poetry but bad; not only verse but prose; and not only material of specific and obvious literary interest, but also fragments of the political and social history which, in this decade more than most, affected the way in which the intelligentsia wrote and thought and behaved.

Already objections buzzed thickly in the air. 'Has Mr Symons heard of a book called *The Long Week-End* or of Malcolm Muggeridge's *The Thirties*, which give us all the discussion we want of the Thirties in this socio-politico-intellectual way? Or if he feels compelled to make his own analysis, why not do it by means of straightforward chapters with headings like "The Influence of Psycho-Analysis on the Early Poetry of W.H. Auden" or, if he is looking for a more popular touch, "Poetry in the Political Melting-Pot"?' Such objections, though, seemed a little beside the point. As a period the Thirties resists analysis: or rather, analysis used in the context of this literary-political movement tends to be a means of ridicule rather than of explanation. It is easy for rationalists to contrast the grandiose intentions of saints and reformers with their frequently pathetic achievements, similarly easy to show the inadequacies and errors of the Thirties artists. It is less easy, but more interesting, to explain why writers in Britain felt themselves necessarily engaged by politics at this time, and what was the aesthetic that imposed a pattern upon

Thirties writing as coherent as the pattern imposed upon the art of the 1890s. 'Its creators are tragically dead, or have made more tragic recantations, for we are patient of every affectation save theirs, and tolerate any artistic heresy save the one they practised thirty years ago.' The words used by A.J.A. Symons of the Nineties art-for-art's-sakers now ring uncomfortably true of the young Left-wing writers whose art was partly a form of mental therapy and partly produced in the service of an imaginary classless future. That future, as the artists of the time conceived it, seems now to be a dream. By revolving the dream perhaps we can see why it looked like reality.

> I am a young man. At least, I am just thirty, and that seems to me young. But more and more for some while now I have been aware of a younger generation than my own growing into manhood and into achievement, and quite lately it has been brought home to me in more than one connection that I really know very little – *very* little – of what these younger men and women think and feel about things. One tends to believe that others of one's age, and younger, agree with one by nature and necessity. But do they? If the Promethean's is, as I take it to be, a genuine youth movement, I hope to learn from them something of that.
>
> Geoffrey West in the *Twentieth Century*
> No. 1, March 1931

Geoffrey West's article, and the Promethean Society to which it refers, were typical of a feeling among young people at the beginning of the Thirties that we were moving into some deeply significant new social and political condition. The Society, an editorial said, 'came spontaneously to life – its birth was not planned, organized, and artificially stimulated by a person or party with a particular axe to grind'. (In fact, it was started as the result of a letter in a weekly paper). And Mr West confirmed that the Promethean movement had no vested interest and made no compromises. 'Above all, I see it as eschewing, to the utmost degree, organization.'

More than two hundred members, most of them young, were quickly gathered, and divided into sectional groups. The Active Peace Group called for 'Disarmament by Example' and for 'the creation of a peace-mind and the utilization of pugnacious instincts for the destruction of social and other evils'. The Sexology Group pronounced its ideal as 'the complete yet reasoned and reasoning liberty of the individual'. The Arts Group wanted 'a nucleus of volunteer writers and research workers who will make it their business to study such problems as, for example, the relations between art and politics, between literature and life, between morality and aesthetics'. 'The two principal motives behind the movement we are supporting are (a) the destruction of certain existing institutions (b) the formation of a new (twentieth century), *Weltanschauung*.' And a Credo in the sixth issue of the *Twentieth Century* called for the creation of a World Commonwealth, with 'the objective as the World State of Mankind governed by regional bodies in constant touch with a central World Directorate, the personnel of which administrative bodies would be chosen for their progressive vision and administrative ability, irrespective of race, region or numerical representation'.

Our first quotations: and with them the inadequacy of simple analysis becomes evident. How naïve and ridiculous are those calls for the creation of a World Commonwealth and of a peace-mind, how long outdated the demand for individual sexual liberty, how solemn the concept of the arts study group: how deliciously comic the idea of achieving these ends while 'eschewing, to the utmost degree, organization'. Yet this modern mockery, like Lytton Strachey's self-conscious awareness of the absurdities in Manning and Arnold, ends by obscuring rather than obliterating the objects against which it is directed, until at last nothing is left but the mocker himself, listening to the sound of his own laughter. The supporters of the Promethean Society were the articulate spearhead of a much larger and less coherent mass of people under thirty who believed that to change the world was not only necessary, but comparatively easy. Probably it would be true to say that at present the form of government in Britain (the paternal Welfare State, whether Tory or Labour) and the forms of sexual conduct (a high degree of personal freedom, limited by the moral sanctions common to those who dwell side by side, television antennae alert, in the new towns, the new flats, the new estates) seem to most people permanent, something that can be destroyed only by nuclear warfare: to the young Public Prometheans, by contrary, it seemed that the society in which they had grown up could not possibly last more than another few years. One good push would bring it down.

The reasons for this belief were rooted in economic and sociological facts. Dr Leavis says somewhere that probably the amount of latent poetical talent is pretty much the same in any period, and the same may be said of latent idealism. The idealism of the young is no more than a jelly of sentiment. Infuse this jelly with the germ of an idea and it sets into a Communist or Fascist. In an extreme situation the young turn naturally to extreme solutions.

> Get there if you can and see the land you once were proud to own,
> Though the roads have almost vanished and the expresses never
> run:
> Smokeless chimneys, damaged bridges, rotting wharves and choked
> canals,
> Tramlines buckled, smashed trucks lying on their side across the
> rails;
> Power-stations locked, deserted, since they drew the boiler fires;
> Pylons fallen or subsiding, trailing dead high-tension wires;
> Head-gears gaunt on grass-grown pit-banks, seams abandoned
> years ago;
> Drop a stone and listen for its splash in flooded dark below.

Auden's vision of a dead country (which also appeared in the first number of the *Twentieth Century*) found its basis in the Labour Government's absolute inability to reduce the number of unemployed much below a figure of three million. Sir Oswald Mosley made quite unsuccessful attempts to move J.H. Thomas, who was charged with reducing unemployment, to some sort of action, and then proposed to the Parliamentary Labour Party schemes involving the extension of pensions and the inauguration of a big programme of public works, to be financed by loans. It was in February 1931, after the complete rejection of Mosley's schemes by the Labour Party that a group of six MPs, five Socialist and one Conservative, refused the Party Whip, and four of the six joined the New Party that was founded under Mosley's leadership. In August a National Government was formed, and the Labour Party was hopelessly divided. In October, *Action*, 'the New Weekly of the New Movement', began its three months' life. Many young people thought that if society was to be changed by Parliamentary means, it must be through some such force as the New Party. They thought also that such a Party, with no organization and little money, could win seats in Parliament, and they found nothing out of the way in Mosley's first editorial:

> We must create a movement which aims not merely at the capture of political power; a movement which grips and transforms

every phase and aspect of national life to post-war purposes; a movement of order, of discipline, of loyalty, but also of dynamic progress; a movement of iron decision, resolution and reality; a movement which cuts like a sword through the knot of the past to the meaning of the modern State. If you would serve such a movement, do it now.

John Strachey, who had been Mosley's PPS, and was one of the founders of the New Party, quickly became alarmed by the creation of a private army of thugs under the guise of a 'Youth Movement', and by Mosley's private praise of Fascism. He resigned in July 1931, but a number of intellectuals still looked kindly on the New Party and were prepared to believe at this time in learning 'from the Nazi movement in Germany' as well as 'from the admirable planning of the Soviets'. Harold Nicolson was the editor of *Action*, and Peter Quennell, Raymond Mortimer, Osbert Sitwell, Alan Pryce-Jones, Christopher Isherwood and Francis Burrell were among the paper's contributors. (Isherwood wrote about 'the Youth Movement in the New Germany'.) But the hope of attaining power, or even wielding political influence, by Parliamentary means, could not survive the October General Election. The New Party failed to win a seat (Mosley got 10,000 votes, but was at the bottom of the poll in Stoke-on-Trent): but much more shattering than this fact, even to most New Party supporters, was the almost complete obliteration of the Labour and Liberal parties. The Labour party was reduced to fifty-one seats, the Liberals to seven. The *Daily Express* heading said: SOCIALISTS WIPED OUT. The Government, with its National Labour and National Liberal allies, had an overall majority of more than 500 seats.

The election of the National Government, which lasted until the war when it was replaced by a coalition of the three main parties, was a watershed in British politics. The path of economic expansion proposed by Mosley (and within a year or two adopted, in very different ways, by Roosevelt in the United States and Hitler in Germany) had been rejected. The economic orthodoxy of the time demanded deflation, which always makes its most savage impact upon the poor. In 1931 the savagery was exercised most obviously through the reduction in unemployment pay, and the establishment of the Means Test.

In August 1931, unemployment pay was 17 shillings a week for a man, 9 shillings for his wife, and 2 shillings for each child. It was thought that the Unemployed Insurance Fund which administered what was always called 'the dole' ought to pay for itself through individual contributions made by those in work and their employers. This dream, however, was not fulfilled, any more than current dreams of a self-supporting railway or Post Office service have any chance of realization. The awkward fact was that there were too many unemployed. What was to be done? Like the idea advanced at present by lunatic theorists that railway and Post Office services should be restricted until they *are* self-supporting (and if the services close down altogether, well, they will have died in a good logical cause), the National Government decided to cut benefits and increase contributions until the human bodies *did* fit the Procrustean bed of theory. The books of the Fund, it was felt, must be made to balance.

The practical result was first to reduce the dole by ten per cent, and then further to limit the number who received it by the Means Test. This confined the period in which the dole would be paid automatically to twenty-six weeks. After that, you had to submit to a Means Test, and if you passed it the dole, now given the label of 'transitional payment', was maintained. Application of the test varied, but it was often brutal and always undignified. In some areas attempts were made to exclude as many people as possible from benefit; under Labour-controlled authorities it was much more easily obtained. Some Public Assistance Committees (called PACs) cut the amount of the payments below the official level, and those thought to be acting too generously were warned, and in some places disciplined.

In the course of the decade things changed slightly. The PACs were replaced by the UAB, the Unemployed Assistance Board. Under what was expected to be the benevolent sway of the UAB, further cuts took place as the lynx-eyed snoopers made reductions for the earnings of sons and daughters. There was a slow and small increase in the amount of the dole, an increase which just about kept pace with rising prices. When the War came the amounts were 17 shillings for a man, 10 shillings for his wife, and 3 shillings for each child.

All this, the manner and measure of it, is hard to imagine for those brought up under the Welfare State. It was impossible not to be aware of the unemployed, although deliberate blindness to the misery of their condition was not uncommon. If you were sacked from a job at any age it was a serious matter, and if you were sacked and over forty your chances of getting work again were small. The atmosphere created was one of cynicism and despair for those who felt that the world they lived in would never change, of revolutionary optimism for those who thought like the young Prometheans.

Many of these optimists believed that the need for extreme solutions had become obvious.

The final condemnation of extreme political views, made by those who disapprove of them for moral or social reasons, is that in Britain such views are not practical; and people who value nothing more than the maintenance of their own positions in society spend a lot of time in demonstrating the errors of sectarianism. But in the Thirties it seemed, almost, that the truth was the reverse of this: that the National Government must be in the Parliamentary saddle for an immeasurable length of time, and that the attempt to overthrow, or even materially affect, the policies of this Government by Parliamentary means was hopeless. Mosley recognized this at once. A few weeks after the election the New Party advocated 'strong Government by a Central Executive of not more than five persons', and within a matter of months the party had become the British Union of Fascists. Very few intellectuals followed Mosley, but they believed, with him, that there was no Parliamentary solution to the problems of Britain. The Labour Party was hopelessly weak, and no new party could hope to capture seats in Parliament. It was plain, then, that the rebirth of Britain must come through chaos and catastrophe. This idea, with sometimes the chaos and catastrophe stressed, sometimes the rebirth, was the basis of the art of the Thirties.

2

Rules for Talking to an Empty Room

Verse will be worn longer this year, and rather Red.
Hugh Gordon Porteus in 1933

Chaos, catastrophe, rebirth: they found expression in the early Thirties in poems like these:

We made all possible preparations,
Drew up a list of firms,
Constantly revised our calculations
And allotted the farms,

Issued all the orders expedient
In this kind of case:
Most, as was expected, were obedient,
Though there were murmurs, of course;

Chiefly against our exercising
Our old right to abuse:
Even some sort of attempt at rising,
But these were mere boys.

For never serious misgiving
Occurred to anyone,
Since there could be no question of living
If we did not win.

The generally accepted view teaches
That there was no excuse,
Though in the light of recent researches
Many would find the cause

In a not uncommon form of terror;
Others, still more astute,
Point to possibilities of error
At the very start.

As for ourselves there is left remaining
Our honour at least,
And a reasonable chance of retaining
Our faculties to the last.

                                        W.H. Auden

Consider these, for we have condemned them;
Leaders to no sure land, guides their bearings lost
Or in league with robbers have reversed the signposts,
Disrespectful to ancestors, irresponsible to heirs.
Born barren, a freak growth, root in rubble,
Fruitlessly blossoming, whose foliage suffocates,
Their sap is sluggish, they reject the sun.

The man with his tongue in his cheek, the woman
With her heart in the wrong place, unhandsome, unwholesome;
Have exposed the new-born to worse than weather,
Exiled the honest and sacked the seer.
These drowned the farms to form a pleasure-lake,
In time of drought they drain the reservoir
Through private pipes for baths and sprinklers.

Getters not begetters; gainers not beginners;
Whiners not winners; no triers, betrayers;
Who steer by no star, whose moon means nothing.
Daily denying, unable to dig:
At bay in villas from blood relations,
Counters of spoons and content with cushions
They pray for peace, they hand down disaster.

They that take the bribe shall perish by the bribe,
Dying of dry rot, ending in asylums,
A curse to children, a charge on the state.
But still their fears and frenzies infect us;
Drug nor isolation will cure this cancer:

It is now or never, the hour of the knife,
The break with the past, the major operation.

C. Day Lewis

Nothing marks the emergence of a literary movement more certainly than a fresh use of words and images, a unity of tone that has
for those inside the movement a particular weight and meaning,
although for those outside the charmed circle it may seem mere
obscurity or affectation. These poems are typical in several ways of
much verse in the early Thirties. In Day Lewis's poem the note of
urgency is sounded through oddities of syntax ('guides their bearings
lost'): language is sharpened by the omission of connectives; the knife
and the major operation at the end are images of violence seen here
as a positive reason for optimism. The technical problem that faced
these poets was that of expressing revolutionary sentiment, which
was something 'new' in English poetry, in some appropriately 'new'
language. A great deal was said at the time about the way in which
images were drawn from pylons and pit-works, from the operation
of machinery, from psychology and science, but really the break with
the verse of the Twenties was sharper than that. The first lines of
Auden's poem are deliberately 'unpoetical', they set out to shock
over-refined sensibilities.

The degree and kind of shock: how can one convey it to those for
whom Auden's work is firmly bound up as 'collected shorter poems'
which have nothing new about them, but are part of the poet's progress through the years towards refinement of language and feeling?
I can remember clearly how deeply significant it seemed to be – and
since it seemed, no doubt was – that Auden and, following him, Day
Lewis (who long ago excluded most of this early work from the canon
of his poetry) and Spender had given up the use of titles, so that
poems were simply numbered I, II, III and onwards to a book's end.
I think this refusal to use titles sprang partly from a wish to discourage
the emphasis placed by anthologies upon the individual poem: the
book that contained the poems, the social attitude expressed in them,
these were the important things. The poets, and those readers sympathetic to them, were looking for unity; titles seemed to imply diver-
sity. But further than this, I am sure it was felt that titles were in
essence romantic, and so to be deprecated.

And through the quads dogmatic words rang clear,
'Good poetry is classic and austere.'

The words were Auden's. It would be hard to over-emphasize the
effect of Auden's personality on other poets in the formative years,
an effect that often found slightly ridiculous expression:

Gain altitude, Auden, then let the base beware!
Migrate, chaste my kestrel, you need a change of air!

C. Day Lewis

There waited for me in the summer morning,
Auden, fiercely. I read, shuddered and knew.

Charles Madge

At Oxford Auden tried to dissuade Spender from the 'weakness'
implied in attending concerts of classical music, and maintained that
'the poet's attitude must be absolutely detached, like that of a surgeon
or scientist'. He might say that his friends should not take him so
seriously, but what he said seemed to be seriously enough intended.

All this is long ago and far away. After some three or four years titles
began to sneak back above the verse printed in magazines, and indeed
their total abandonment had a distinct flavour of that absurdity noted
by Max Beerbohm in Enoch Soames's feeling that he should leave
his book of poems untitled ('If,' [Rothenstein] urged, 'I went into a
bookseller's and said simply "Have you got?" or "Have you a copy
of?" how would they know what I wanted?'). Auden has given titles
to those early poems of his, titles often most unhappily facetious, and
the attempt to move towards classicism and austerity must now seem
to many of the poets of that time a rash excess of youth. 'We are all
romantic today,' so we might adapt Sir William Harcourt: and no
doubt it is true that the production of classical art implies an accepted
critical canon, a deep calm at the heart of society. Instead of such a
canon we have a new art movement every ten years, instead of calm
we have continual storms, each one threatening to wash away our
habits, our beliefs, our very forms of life. How can our art be anything
but romantic, subjective, passionately individual? Yet the abandonment of the classical position, or mock-classical position, was in its

way tragic: reading again those early poems of Auden's, and some other poems written during the first years of the Thirties, one feels again the old shock of excitement. They promise something that time and society and human weakness have denied.

The shock is incommunicable, then: but I think it should be possible for any reader to see that Auden's *Poems* (1930) and *The Orators* (1932) belong to that small class of works which have an absolute importance and value at the time of their publication because they express cohesively a set of attitudes which have been waiting for an expositor. There have been one or two such books, not necessarily masterpieces or even works of high talent, in every decade of the twentieth century. Kingsley Amis's *Lucky Jim* was such a book, expressive of that faintly Philistine no-nonsense barbarian common-sense which, as we can see now, marked a whole generation of writers in the Fifties. The sense of encountering something new that was felt by many readers of *Lucky Jim* was similar to the feeling one had in reading Auden's *Poems*. It would be wrong to say that this feeling had no aesthetic basis, but it was not primarily aesthetic. What one felt, as nearly as such things can be put into crude words, was: 'Here is somebody who expresses what I believe myself, but have never been able to say.' The atmosphere of schoolboy plotting, the heartiness, the assonances and half-rhymes, all these were wonderfully refreshing after the dryness of Eliot and his imitators; the frequent references to science and psychoanalysis found a response in our vague awareness of these things; and, pushing deeper, there was something profoundly congenial in Auden's idea that 'love' was not adequate in itself, was even somehow wrong:

> You whom I gladly walk with, touch,
> Or wait for as one certain of good,
> We know it, we know that love
> Needs more than the admiring excitement of union....
> Needs death, death of the grain, our death,
> Death of the old gang

Looking back, I think that the especial appeal of Auden's attitude was the combination of swaggering certainty and doubt, of poetry exceptionally difficult in syntax and meaning put beside other verse of rollicking simplicity.

Beethameer, Beethameer, bully of Britain,
With your face as fat as a farmer's bum;
Though you pose in private as a playful kitten
Though the public you poison are pretty well dumb,
They shall turn on their betrayer when the time is come.
The cousins you cheated shall recover their nerve
And give you the thrashing you richly deserve.

Auden was followed closely by Day Lewis:

Scavenger barons and your jackal vassals,
Your pimping press-gang, your unclean vessels,
We'll make you swallow your words at a gulp
And turn you back to your element, pulp.
Don't bluster, Bimbo, it won't do you any good;
We can be much ruder and we're learning to shoot.
Closet Napoleon, you'd better abdicate,
You'd better quit the country before it's too late.

That was the voice of arrogant certainty, almost unintelligible to those who do not remember the political and social influence that press lords wielded, or tried to wield, in the Thirties, when Lord Rothermere's *Daily Mail* enthusiastically supported Italian and German Fascism, and Lord Beaverbrook's *Daily Express* pursued for years an Empire Crusade. But beside this voice certain of victory was another that expected death or defeat:

All leave is cancelled to-night; we must say good-bye
We entrain at once for the North; we shall see in the morning
The headland we're doomed to attack; snow down to the tide-line:
Though the bunting signals
'Indoors before it's too late; cut peat for your fires',
We shall lie out there.

The personality and poetic power of Auden moulded a whole climate of feeling: yet what was called 'the Auden Group' never really existed, for of his contemporaries Day Lewis was the only writer stylistically affected by him, and it was upon writers a few years younger than himself that Auden's style and attitude had a really stunning effect. In the aesthetic, the theory of art's place in society, that was painfully worked out by writers during the decade, Auden's contribution was upon the whole a pessimistic one, concerned with catastrophe. What most of his poems seemed to be saying was that society must be changed, and that the artist could and should play a leading part in changing it. Yet to be a poet was in itself somehow a mark of inadequacy: the young (and poets at this time were deeply concerned with youth), happy and psychologically stable, would have no need of poetry:

> Give them spontaneous skill at holding rein,
> At twisting dial, or at making fun,
> That these may never need our craft,
> Who, awkward, pasty, feeling the draught,
> Have health and skill and beauty on the brain.

Love itself needed for its proper existence 'our death, Death of the old gang', and in many poems Auden emphasized the contradiction between individual love and the universal, rather impersonal love that would succeed it in the new society. In several poems, too, the death of heroic rebels was foreseen before ultimate victory: and it would be fair to say that the death was more important to Auden than the victory.

With the pleasure that we took in Auden's ambiguity went the sense that he was socially an extremely slippery customer. His poetry served as a sort of enormous magnifying glass through which we could examine our own doubts with the fascinated horror that one feels in looking at an enlargement of a slight deformity; and with our admiration went a good deal of head shaking. I was amused to read in Richard Hoggart's brilliant book about Auden that 'In *The Orators* the important figure of the Airman symbolizes the forces of release and liberation': amused because I remembered how anxiously this point was debated immediately after the book's publication. Was not the Airman, we asked ourselves, a Fascist?

> The few shall be taught who want to understand,
> Most of the rest shall love upon the land;
> Living in one place with a satisfied face
> All of the women and most of the men
> Shall work with their hands and not think again.

Were not these Fascist sentiments? Didn't Auden clearly approve of them? And the very things about the Airman that Hoggart chooses for praise: 'He experiences that sense of control which comes from the ability to trace some pattern in the mess which, to those involved below, seems overwhelming', seemed to us most dubious virtues. Was it possible to reconcile this idea of a healer coming down from above with a concept of social justice? All this seems absurd, no doubt it does, in a time when the author of *The Orators* (who has not lost the trick of ambiguity) calls the book 'a fair notion fatally injured'. Yet I think it is true to say that the Airman remains a highly ambiguous figure, and that the conception of him as a Fascist was not simply foolish. In their place and time the arguments were important even though we may say now, with the wisdom of hindsight, that Auden's changes of stance and hesitations are qualities that help to keep his early poetry viable, when so much other verse and prose of the time has crumbled away.

I have never understood why *New Signatures*, the little verse anthology published in 1932, has been regarded by most critics of the period as a landmark. In it Michael Roberts included a few poems by Auden, Spender and Day Lewis, but more by such writers as William Empson, A.S.J Tessimond and Julian Bell, who had little to do with the Thirties movement. *New Country*, which appeared in the following year, is a much more characteristic collection, both in its excesses and in its earnest gropings towards something new.

> I think, and the writers in this book obviously agree, that there is only one way of life for us: to renounce that system (monopoly capitalism) now and to live by fighting against it.... But if you, reader, stand for the accepted order; if you cannot envisage a state in which resources are used to meet the needs of the community and not for individual profit, please remember that the Union Jack, the British Grenadiers, and cricket are not your private property. They are ours. Your proper emblem is a balance sheet. You're a fool if you think your system will give you cricket much longer. Haven't you realised? *Cricket doesn't pay.* If you want cricket you'd better join us.
>
> Michael Roberts

He will go to the small club behind the Geisha Café. He will ask whether there is a meeting to-night. At first he may be regarded with suspicion, even taken for a police spy. And quite naturally. He will have to prove himself, to prove that he isn't a mere neurotic, an untrustworthy freak. It will take time. But it is the only hope. He will at least have made a start.

Edward Upward

The first quotation is from Michael Roberts's introduction to the book, the second is the end of an experimental short story about going home to lodgings for Sunday lunch, in which the narrator, speaking sometimes in the first person and sometimes in the third, attacks those who try to 'deny history'. History resides at present in 'the vulgarity and shallowness of the town's attempts at art and entertainment, in the apprehensive dreariness of your Sunday leisure'. But history will not always mean this. History is going to live with those who 'are going to destroy the more obvious material causes of misery in the world'. History is down at the club behind the Geisha Café.

History is on our side. The sentiment is at the heart of a hundred poems. It expresses the conviction which led many writers to view the future with complete assurance. 'The certainty of new life must be your starting-point,' Day Lewis says in his 'Letter to a Young Revolutionary' in the same volume, and the new life meant a new form of society. The belief that history is on one side or another is a heady one. Its import would be better conveyed by inversion, by saying *We are on history's side.* History is conceived nominally as an inevitable process of human development, physical and mental: really as a person or god, an abstraction made real, in very much the shape of that Christian God who was denied by many of these young writers. And just as the expression of belief in God seemed mere commonsense four hundred years ago, even to those who lacked faith, so, it is implied by Michael Roberts, it is the part of ordinary wisdom to get on to history's band wagon. History, like God in the past, is a certain winner; and once on the band wagon you can be promised almost anything with confidence. Do you want to play cricket? More to the point, do you want your son to play cricket? Do you want to make England into 'a land of milk and honey, of crops and cattle, not a string of hotels and "beauty spots"'? (Day Lewis). To enjoy sexual freedom, make a new society and a new art? Then you had better join us, for this personally-incarnated history intends to do all of these things.

Nothing is more curious than the disparity between the tone of absolute certainty in which these revolutionary sentiments were uttered, and the actual situation. One might think that Michael Roberts, Day Lewis, Upward, Auden, were members of some great revolutionary party, that their books were read in tens of thousands, that a situation existed similar to that of the July days in Russia, with the hour of the knife and the major operation quite obviously at hand. Not at all. The number of unemployed remained static, Fascism gained more adherents, the National Government sat with monumental firmness in the saddle. The writers were merely showing their prescience and sensibility, expressing the widespread feeling already noticed, that the form of society in which they had grown up could not possibly last. These lists of firms and allotting of farms, these condemnations of political leaders and press barons, these last-chance warnings about the British Grenadiers and cricket, were largely addressed by the writers to each other. This was not always so. Within three or four years, at the height of the Popular Front, a large audience existed for the popular radical verse that several members of the Auden Group talked about: but at the time when Auden and Day Lewis, in particular, were making such threatening noises about what lay in store in the future, their audience was very small.

Auden was by general consent the leader of these poets: the most discussed, the most admired, the most read. The figures of his sales are of some interest. His first publicly printed book, *Poems*, was issued in paper wrappers in 1930. The edition was one of 1,000 copies, and the book was sold at half a crown. In spite of the fact that Auden's long poem, 'Paid On Both Sides' had been printed in T.S. Eliot's *The Criterion* (which, although it was the most famous and influential periodical of the time, had at no time a circulation of more than 800 copies), and in spite of the furore that attended the publication of *New Signatures*, this impression was not exhausted until 1933. In November of that year the book was published in boards, in an edition of 1,000 copies, and in September 1934, it was reprinted in another edition of 1,500 copies. The next reprint, of 1,517 copies, came in 1937. *The Orators* was published in 1932 in an edition of 1,000 copies. A second edition of another 1,000 copies was published in September 1934, and no reprint was called for until September 1943.

By the end of 1933 (and it is of this time that I am writing) Auden's *Poems* had sold rather more than 1,000 copies. *The Orators* rather less than that number. This is not said in denigration of Auden (very likely the sales of other poets were smaller still), but to point the difference between the sort of language used in the poems and the number of people listening to it. To one sort of artist, of course, the size of the audience doesn't matter, but to those deeply conscious of the artist's entanglement with society it is vitally important. One does at times have an uncomfortable feeling that these young writers were laying down rules for talking to an empty room.

3

The Old School and the
New Freedom

Christopher Isherwood's *Lions and Shadows* is a key that at first glance
seems to unlock doors that most people keep firmly shut. We turn
the key, the door opens. It is disconcerting to find that we are not in
a room at all, but in a long corridor decorated with mementoes of –
well, of all things, the public schools and universities attended by Mr
Isherwood and his friends Mr Chalmers, Mr Weston, Mr Linsley,
Mr Savage. We hurry along the corridor – there will be time later
on for looking at these interesting relics – to find another door at the
end of it. And this door resists our key. We turn back to the school
blazers, the jokes, the pictures of the author's friends wearing false
beards and moustaches. It is fun to look at them, even if in one or
two cases the disguise is teasingly difficult to pierce, but we had hoped
for something more.

Take, for instance, a couple of lines from a poem in *The Orators*:

Where is the trained eye? Under the sofa.
Where is Moxon? Dreaming of nuns.

Who is Moxon? The poem offers no answer, but we learn from
Lions and Shadows that Moxon, Reynard Moxon, is one of the characters in a game played by Isherwood and his friend Chalmers, otherwise Edward Upward, in which an imaginary village called Mortmere
was created and peopled, as the Brontës peopled their imaginary
Angria. Moxon is a villain, who owns a large black serpent which
goes with him for rambles after dark. His appearance is notable, 'that
nonchalant yet rapid stride, the scarcely visible limp, the wooden
action of the pointed shoulder, the inert hand carelessly flashing with
its five diamond rings'. Explanations may be found in the book of
other phrases in Auden's poems: we learn incidentally that one phrase
comes directly from remarks made about cutting bread at prep school,

and another is taken from the Norse Sagas. This is the sort of thing that is lying about in the corridor, but we want to know more, we want to ask how a poet can justify private jokes about figures like Moxon, and what Mortmere meant in terms of Isherwood's own personality. The answers to these questions lie behind the second locked door. *Lions and Shadows* is lively, subtle, fresh, but it offers no more than an illusion of frankness. It is significant that although Isherwood was thirty-four years old when the book was published, it seems to have been written by a man ten years younger.

The difference between Angria and Mortmere is that the Brontës took their Gondals seriously, while to Isherwood and Chalmers the villains and fools of Mortmere, the discovery of enemies in Cambridge shop assistants and college waiters and the invention of 'the Other Town' which led out of Cambridge through 'a little old door in a high blank wall', are all (how could they be anything else?) three-quarters joke. And the joke is always intruding upon things they mean to treat seriously: so Moxon makes his wicked entrances into Auden's poems, so Upward's narrator finds his way not to a trade union meeting but to the small club behind the Geisha Café, so a predominant image for all these writers is that of the frontier. What fun everything is on this side of the frontier, how deliciously cosy it is to be with friends who talk one's own sort of serio-comic nonsense: yet on the other side life, as it seems, is going on. On the other side, the myth of the future: on ours, the myth of Mortmere.

Great literature can be made out of any myth, as Yeats's gyres show, but it is a prime requisite that the myth must correspond to something which the artist takes with the deepest, most reverent seriousness. The most damaging criticism that can be made of Isherwood and his friends is that their deepest desires and longings were connected with public school and university; that, wishing to speak in popular language to a mass of people, they found themselves talking to each other in the language of their public schools. If it had been possible to penetrate that final room, it is likely that we should have found there an ideal image of school life:

> The clock strikes ten, the tea is on the stove,
> And up the stair come voices that I love.
> Strength, satisfaction, force, delight,
> To these players of badminton to-night,
> To Favel, Holland, sprightly Alexis, give.

Like the family album, this book will, I hope, be superficially more funny than tragic, for so odd a system of education does not demand a pompous memorial.... Whatever the political changes in this country during the next few years one thing surely is almost certain: the class distinctions will not remain unaltered and the public school, as it exists today, will disappear.

Graham Greene, *The Old School*, 1934

The idea that every attitude contains its opposite is strikingly illustrated in the extraordinary concern felt by the intelligentsia with the public schools in the Thirties. The public schools, it was said, were utterly barbarous and reactionary, had no place at all in any possible future society; they inculcated standards of behaviour quite inappropriate to the modern world; history was not on their side; in a sense, what the intelligentsia wanted more than anything else in the Thirties was freedom from the principles endorsed by the authorities at public schools. Stephen Spender, after being caned at his preparatory school by a headmaster who said 'I think now I understand you', comments: 'We had, of course, deeply and instinctively realized that the headmaster was sadistic. It would have surprised my parents to have known that they might just as well have had me educated at a brothel for flagellants as at the school referred to, but it was so, and I am sure it is equally true of many other preparatory schools.'

When boys were not being beaten they were being watched to see that they had no sex relations with each other. In Graham Greene's school there were no locks on the lavatory doors. And when headmasters were not sadistic, they were silly. P.B.H. Lyon, headmaster of Rugby, discussed sex in a solemn article in *The Spectator* on 'What you ought to tell Kenneth before he goes back to his old school':

Kenneth will, I believe, instinctively shy at the first suggestion of 'smut'; what you can do is to reassure him that such aversion is not cowardice, that nothing noble or manly lies along that road. But this is not enough; innocence must be reinforced by knowledge of the right kind, before knowledge of the wrong kind overpowers it.... For myself, I think a boy's house-master should add this to his many duties; let us hope 'Fishface' (an imaginary housemaster) thinks the same. He would do it well, being (as I had said) a kind and sensible man, who has probably expounded these mysteries to innumerable small boys in his time.

'You recognize the old idea,' Mr Greene comments. 'Sex is dirty, but if it's called marriage, it's much too sacred to be talked about in public.'

Yet together with this distaste and contempt for public school standards went very often the feeling that one had had splendid times at school, and that the authorities could not be blamed for their attitude. 'The mass production of gentlemen is their *raison d'être*, and one can hardly suggest that they should adopt principles which would destroy them,' said Auden, at this time himself a schoolmaster; and he suggested, not quite seriously, that the number of professional teachers should be very small. 'The rest would be conscripted, every citizen after some years in the world would be called up to serve his two or three years teaching for the State, after which he would return to his job again.' Commenting on the 'honour system' at his own school, Gresham's, by which every new boy was made to promise not to swear, smoke, or say or do anything indecent, and to promise also that if he saw any other boy breaking these promises he would first try to persuade him to report the error to his housemaster, and if he refused would report him personally, Auden admits that the system worked, but identifies it with Fascism. 'The best reason I have for opposing Fascism is that at school I lived in a Fascist state'. It is a reason that is interesting principally because it shows the importance to Auden of public school life.

In no other decade of the century could such a novel as Arthur Calder-Marshall's *Dead Centre* have been written: a book consisting simply of some fifty short autobiographical narratives, of which the purpose is to give a total picture of public school life. *Dead Centre* was much praised as an original *avant-garde* novel, but the most curious thing about it was Calder-Marshall's extraordinary absorption in the minutiae of public school life, the attempt to render quite flatly its characteristic tone.

I'd been waiting for some time for Podmore to give himself away. As a boy, he's intolerable, an intellectual prig, as bad as Peele, without half his ability. He once said to me, 'Which do you prefer, sir, Puccini or Donizetti?' Think of it, that was when he was a new boy. I answered, 'I prefer spaghetti' which I thought was rather neat.

Those members of the intelligentsia who came of age in the late Twenties generally wanted little more than reform of the public schools. Spender, upon the whole, was happy at UCS, William Plomer asked only that games be treated less seriously than they were at Rugby ('At my school I received the impression that the ritual of the cricket field, more elaborate and just a trifle more sincerely performed than that of the chapel, was equally religious'), and that boys 'should not be pestered or brutalized with irrelevant drudgery and petty tyranny'. But to those a few years younger, such projected reforms seemed mere feeble pruning of a poisonous growth. Giles and Esmond Romilly, schoolboys at Wellington at the beginning of the Thirties, identified this very 'progressiveness' as the most sinister thing about the public schools.

Once advanced beyond the 'wise imperialism' of the Headmaster, or the liberalism of most of the staff, once dare to show yourself in a black homburg or a red tie – clothes being, if anything, more important than politics in England – and you became anti-social, a menace to be watched and checked. For the 'enemy' in public schools, the reactionary element against which this book is directed, is no longer a 'stolid' conservatism, but a 'progressive' liberalism ... In criticising the public schools, it is essential to bear in mind the part they play in relation to capitalist society, to see how all their teaching, the emphasis on games, for instance, is conditioned by the economic motives of the middle class.

At Wellington the Romillys went beyond wearing black homburgs. They had Communist literature sent to them, and induced thirty boys to wear the badge of the Anti-War Movement instead of poppies, on Armistice Day. Together they edited a magazine called *Out of Bounds*, which bore on the front cover of the first issue the words 'Against Reaction in the Public Schools'. The paper, 'written exclusively for the Public Schools, by schoolboys', opposed the OTC, propagandist history teaching, games worship, the official attitude towards sex, and 'the suppression of left-wing opinion'. Several schools, including Wellington, banned the paper. It included articles on sex ('Sex at – was a consolation and amusement'), on the 'voluntary' nature of the OTC, on corporal punishment, on masturbation. ('No healthy boy over-masturbates, because it's much too boring for one thing, while a rest pause between erections is a physiological necessity.')

It is not so much the nature of the criticism as the passionate
fervour with which it was expressed, the intensity with which the
youthful members of the intelligentsia wrote about their public school
experiences, the loving hatred they felt for the games-playing heroes,
that today seems strangest. Their attitude is summed up in a conversation between George Orwell and John Strachey, at a time when
Strachey had been attacking the public schools, root and branch:

Orwell You have a small son. Where will he go to school?
J.S.   By the time he is old enough for us to worry about that, I
          hope that the whole system will have been destroyed.
Orwell But supposing it still exists. Where will you send him?
J.S.   If the system still exists as it is at present?
Orwell Yes.
J.S.   To Eton. It's the best education we have.

Orwell was deeply shocked.

Conscious revolt against a society's standards, unconscious acceptance of them: what this meant in practice was the demand for unlimited individual freedom. It was at this point that the public school
intellectuals of 'the Auden Group', with their private jokes and con-
spiratorial games, met the earnest seekers after political and sexual
liberation (comparatively few of whom came from public schools)
who belonged to the Promethean Society or contributed to *The Adelphi*.
Each successive decade of our century has had its own form of social
liberation, and always it has involved a drastic break with the
immediate past. In the early Thirties the concept of 'freedom'
appeared an absolute good. It was thought more important that children should develop as free personalities than that they should receive
formal education, and the ideals embodied in Neill's Summerhill
School became fashionable. People began conscientiously to assert
'the complete yet reasoned and reasoning rights of the individual'.
Since marriage was a bourgeois and immoral institution it was mere
commonsense for people in love to live together; the sexual act was
acknowledged to be not merely natural, but pleasurable for both
partners; the limits put upon what was acknowledged as sexual cus-
tom were greatly enlarged. The Thirties might also be called the
homosexual decade, in the sense that in these years homosexuality

became accepted as a personal idiosyncrasy: and became, too, a sort
of password, so that several homosexual writers of little talent found
their work accepted by magazines simply on a basis of personal
friendship. It would probably be untrue to say that any writer of
heterosexual instincts suffered seriously through this homosexual
literary tendency among the young, but the assessment of writers on
the basis of their sexual attractiveness can hardly be anything but
damaging to literary standards.

About all this, it may seem, there is nothing specifically *new*. People
lived together in the Twenties without benefit of marriage lines, and
A, B and C, those well-known homosexual writers, were firmly established with their young men for years before the Thirties. That is
true enough: the unique contribution made by the intelligentsia in
the Thirties to the change in our sexual ethic rested in the attitude
they adopted, by which the assertion of sexual freedom appeared to
be a social duty. 'It would be possible to read Mr Lyon,' Graham
Greene says, 'without ever guessing that sexual intercourse was pleas-
ant or amusing.' In the Thirties the acknowledgement of pleasure
was there, sure enough, but part of it came from the sense that social
or sexual conventions were being defied. It would be an exaggeration
to envisage thousands of young men and women in suburban bed-
sitting rooms setting out to practise some of the variations described
in the *Encyclopædia of Sexual Knowledge* by Dr A. Costlar (who was, as
we now know, Arthur Koestler): an exaggeration, yes, but one with
much metaphorical truth in it, in the sense that experiment, in life
as in art, seemed a vital necessity. During the war comparative strangers slept with each other quite casually, as the natural sequel to
visiting a theatre or missing the last train home, but in the Thirties
precept could never be put into practice with such unselfconscious
simplicity. Every illicit sexual act seemed a blow struck in aid of an
ideal theoretical freedom.

4

The Pyramid

There is, or at least there should be, a large card stuck up above my desk, a warning of dangers and responsibilities. NO LIT CRIT, the card says firmly, and just beneath it, NO HINDSIGHT. Below are more positive instructions: *The approach historico-materialistico-journalistico-sociologico-autobiographico. The style, easy. Avoid guilt-feeling. Define all terms.*

This, I am afraid, is Thirtyish humour, out of date.

It isn't easy to write easily, or to avoid the perilous ascent to literary criticism, or to escape hindsight. It was my firm intention when I started to quote only from pieces actually written in the Thirties, since all reminiscence, all glances back in exultation, anger or misgiving, are revelations of the writer's feelings in the present and not in the past: but it is not possible to write about Spain (for instance) without using the revelations made by Arthur Koestler in his autobiography, which illustrate so clearly the way in which idealism and generosity were deliberately and cynically *used*. This sort of hindsight, now that I reconsider, seems essential to the theme. There is a double danger in using it: that of seeming smugly knowledgeable years after the event, and the contrary danger of profitless breast-beating ('How could I have been so deceived...'). With the abysses on either side noted, it may be that the tightrope of hindsight can be successfully trodden. I meant also to avoid literary criticism as such, since it is not the object of a book like this to make a new assessment of Auden's poems: but, in trying to show artists in relation to the pressures of their time, I have found myself writing – what shall I call it? – socio-literary criticism. This, too, seems inevitable, and this, too, must be confined within its socio-literary straitjacket.

Define all terms: what about that uneasy one, intelligentsia?

The term remains obstinately fluid, in spite, of Arthur Koestler's attempt in an article to give it a history and a shape. It is a hybrid word, and an ugly one: but still a word uncommonly convenient, because each separate user gives it an individual meaning. 'The class consisting of the educated portion of the population and considered as capable of forming public opinion,' says my edition of the *Shorter Oxford*: but I don't believe the word is often used strictly in that sense, and it is certainly not the sense in which I used it in the last chapter. I meant there, and mean hereafter, to include among the intelligentsia both the hard core of genuine artists of all kinds and in all mediums, and the massive soft outer flesh of those with vague artistic aspirations which find no more public expression than a liking for Swedish furniture, membership of a film society, the production of a dozen poems kept in a locked drawer. There were perhaps a million people of this sort in Britain during the Thirties, people who sometimes bought books that were favourably reviewed in the Sunday papers, read poets in anthologies rather than in collected volumes, liked the Impressionists but knew that it was fashionable to admire Picasso; people who, in spite of their shortcomings and their snobberies, believed sincerely that works of art were the fine flowers of a civilization whose proper glory was free speech. It is these people who in Britain have been the chief support of art and artists since the Industrial Revolution, and when I write of the intelligentsia it is their collective face, the features shapeless and sexless but fixed in a smile of liberal goodwill, that I see.

Such liberal goodwill stopped far short, for most of them, of any serious interest in politics, yet with Hitler's accession to power in 1933 and the tide of Fascism rising in almost every European country, it was these people who found themselves part of a national movement both political and artistic: a movement designed to stop Fascism through speeches, sanctions, letters of protest, the League of Nations, the Peace Pledge Union, the Anti-War League. This intelligentsia, as the social and political situation, at home and abroad, became more threatening, provided an audience for the 'revolutionary' middle-class poets, who found their attack upon the decay of British society and their satire on the standards of suburban bourgeois life appreciated by – why, by the enlightened members of that very suburban middle class. Edmund Wilson once said that the poets of 'the Auden Group' found verse turning to prose in their hands, as Alice found the croquet mallets turning to flamingos; it would be true also to say that they found the ideal working-class audience of their imagination turning in disconcerting fact to groups of middle-class aesthetes, sociologists and do-gooders.

The political-artistic movement of the Thirties thus slowly took the form of a pyramid. The broad base was formed by the million-strong intelligentsia, who may for convenience be called the Audience. Above them was a group perhaps 50,000 strong, of people who read some of the little magazines in which new writers were first published, and actually bought some of their books. This section of the pyramid was much younger than the base, and its social composition was complex. It included working-class intellectuals, who believed that the proletarian novel and theatre were the coming art forms, but considered the work of bourgeois poets as of some temporary interest; members of the lower middle class − that is, those who had been educated at state or grammar schools, and in many cases had gone on to red brick universities; and a considerable number of professional men and women, doctors, scientists, teachers, lawyers, architects, dons, economists, who were looking for a link between art and society. This is in many ways the most interesting part of the pyramid, for in its members were the seeds of the shifting pattern of the decade, and even of the post-war Welfare State. Since these people had in many cases the practical ability and organizing energy that artists lack, they played a large part in making the theatre and the novel, and to a less degree painting and music, vehicles for social propaganda. It was from this middle part of the pyramid, rather than from the artists themselves, that there came all those exhortations about moving out of the ivory tower of the imagination into the market place. In the sense that all artists are to some degree concerned with the form of their work, with the mould into which their ideas are poured, these people were enemies of art, since they were almost always impatient of merely formal considerations: but in another aspect they were, at this time of social flux, a powerful energizing force. Let us call them the Pragmatists.

Certainly the Pragmatists were felt to be useful by the Artists themselves, perhaps a thousand of them, who lived precariously at the top of the pyramid. At this point of time, the time of Hitler's triumph in Germany and just afterwards, the poets were the most articulate of them: the social realist novels, the documentary slices of life, the realistic or surrealistic paintings, were to come.

The image of the pyramid is, naturally, too simple, for its three parts were not detached but continually interpenetrative, with people from the Audience flowing up into the Pragmatic section, and Pragmatists occasionally moving into the comparatively rarefied air at the top. Too simple, but still useful: as the decade goes on we shall see the Artists taking nourishment from their roots in the Audience, and at the same time adapting themselves to the Audience's habits and standards. The revolutionary shoots will change their character, and develop into buds of middle-class nonconformity. The Pragmatists in the middle, ideally all readers of the *New Statesman*, will boil away like geysers, frothing anger at the Audience for its smug liberalism and at the Artists for their social inadequacy. And still the pyramid, in spite of its dissonant parts and its changing form, will remain stuck together: its coherent gum the threat of Fascism.

The shock caused by the success of German Fascism ran through the whole of liberal society in Britain. Today we regard violent nationalism as something normal, and are given to excusing its 'excesses' by our knowledge that excesses are committed also on the other side. No doubt the Algerians are terrorists: are not the French also terrorists? Do they not use torture as a matter of course? For the matter of that, are not torture and brutality used by all nations against inconvenient minorities? These things appear to us as truisms – it would be unrealistic, we say, not to accept as a fact that the torture chamber and the labour camp, so far from being exceptional, are used when necessary by all nations as instruments of policy. To believe anything else, to think that human affairs can ever be ordered by a liberal dream of reason, seems mere hypocrisy. But this was not always so. At the beginning of the Thirties it was a tenet of faith for the Audience that reason was slowly replacing force in the conduct of human affairs, that all political and social problems could be solved through the League of Nations, and that in Germany the Weimar Republic, enlightened, reasonable, tolerant of homosexuals and other sexual deviants, prepared always to educate rather than to punish, was in many ways a model for other Governments. The Republic's miserable collapse before the forces of Fascism was the greatest single shock endured by the Audience during the whole decade.

Documentation of the outrages committed by German Fascism came quickly, and it would probably be true to say that the acts themselves seemed less appalling than the deliberate degradation of the small Jewish minority among the German people. The destruction of Jewish art, the ruin and torture of Jewish people, carried out in the service of a 'pure' nationalism, seemed almost incredible to the liberal mind: and worst of all was the fact that these measures were plainly successful, that Fascism had for many German people an appeal never possessed by the Weimar Republic, that no League of Nations could legislate against it successfully. Where liberal beliefs ended, the consciousness of struggle began.

Who live under the shadow of a war,
What can I do that matters?
My pen stops, and my laughter, dancing, stop
Or ride to a gap.

To the question asked by Stephen Spender in one of his early poems, the Audience and the Pragmatists found two answers: the first, that of collective resistance to Fascism, the second, that of Pacifism.

5

The Coming Struggle for Power

In October 1934, Canon 'Dick' Sheppard invited men who cared for peace to send him a postcard. The card was to say: 'I renounce war, and I will never support or sanction another.' Why should such an invitation be resisted? To what, after all, did it commit you beyond the act of posting a card? Within a year 80,000 people had renounced war, and the Peace Pledge Union had been founded by those who had signed a pledge which, when war came, was honoured no more than are most temperance pledges. Most of those who joined the Peace Pledge Union, however, did so in the belief that if they gathered enough members war would become impossible. There could be no doubt that the movement was an enormous success. It was given impetus by the Peace Ballot, undertaken originally by the League of Nations Union.

Peace Weeks were held, a journal called *Peace News* appeared, big demonstrations in favour of peace through negotiation took place in most unlikely spots. Two thousand people took part in a peace march through Bury, the Rex Cinema in Norbury was packed tight with an audience of 1,600, while crowds clamoured for admission at the doors. In November 1937, the Peace Pledge Union had 133,000 members organized into 725 groups, and when two young men were sacked by a firm of Lloyd's underwriters for wearing white as well as red poppies on Armistice Day, the *News Chronicle* sounded a warning: 'The firm's attitude savours of Fascism.'

A comprehensive survey of the Thirties would undoubtedly have to consider in detail the activities of the Peace Pledge Union, but their interest from the point of view of this book is confined to showing the reaction of the Artists and Pragmatists for whom *peace* became almost as dirty a word as *war*. The positions taken up are well conveyed in two pamphlets, Aldous Huxley's presentation of the case for Pacifism, *What Are You Going To Do About It?*, and Day Lewis's reply, *We Are Not Going To Do Nothing*. It was necessary, Huxley said, for 'at least one government of an important sovereign state' to act

pacifistically towards its neighbours, and it was the immediate practical task of pacifists to see that this was their own government. He
attacked the middle-class revolutionaries:

> How do you propose to change the existing system? By violence,
> say the revolutionaries. But if violence is used as the means, the
> end achieved will inevitably be different from the end proposed.
> The pacifist does not object to the ends originally proposed by
> the revolutionaries; on the contrary, he regards such ends as being
> intrinsically desirable. What he rejects is the means by which the
> revolutionaries set out to realize these ends.... If Communism is
> to be achieved it can only be achieved by non-violent means.

The arguments are familiar. They are seen here in a conveniently
simplified form, and the arguments by Day Lewis in his reply have
the same sort of cartoon simplification:

> Let us put a question of simple arithmetic before Mr Huxley.
> How is humanity better served, by using violence to restrain one
> gangster from killing ten citizens, or by allowing the one gangster
> to live and the ten citizens to die? Let Mr Huxley imagine himself
> standing by the gangster with the machine-gun and reflect what
> he would do in the two or three seconds before the gun was to be
> fired on ten of his friends. Would he not do a little 'evil' to secure
> a great 'good'? Would he not for a moment allow himself to forget
> that his 'means' were contaminated, and think more of the justice
> of his 'end'?
> The question we should ask ourselves is not: 'Is violence jus-
> tified?' but 'Will the use of violence in this particular concrete
> situation benefit the majority of persons concerned?'

The justification of violence sprang originally, of course, from the
theoreticians of Communism, but for many young people it came
from John Strachey's book, *The Coming Struggle for Power*.

Just as Auden's poems were a sparking point for the imaginations of
the Artists, so Strachey's book, published in 1932, embodied a code
of belief and conduct for most of the Pragmatists, and a considerable
section of the Audience. The idea of a struggle for power was deeply

congenial to them, since there was nothing that they disliked more than the idea of gradual change: and Strachey's lucid blend of popular Marxism and humanism had the force of a vision:

The capitalist system is dying and cannot be revived.... Religion, literature, art, science, the whole of the human heritage of knowledge will be transformed. And the new forms, whether higher or lower, which these principal concepts of man's imagination will assume, will depend on what new economic system will succeed the capitalist system.

Strachey's greatest appeal lay in his application of Marxist ideas to the history of Britain. Wars were seen as simply 'a struggle for the market' and the war against Napoleon was won because 'Britain's economy was sufficiently strong, owing to its imperial profits, not only to keep an army for five years in Spain, but to pay enormous subsidies to her European allies'. The structure of capitalism was 'adapted to an age of individualism and "freedom" alone', and this age was almost over. There were only two social forms that could possibly replace this individualistic capitalism, Fascism and Communism, and 'the leaders of the Labour Party are at present using all their powers to ensure that the workers should be so powerless, so castrated, that a fascist dictatorship would be the inevitable result'. In this view, the psychological function of the Social Democratic parties throughout Europe was to 'satisfy the workers' need to dream of Socialism, whilst remaining tied to capitalism. And they do this with great skill'. The only method by which human civilization could be maintained at all, then, was Communism: and for those who averted their eyes from the Soviet Union, who cried out about inevitable harshnesses and rigidities and limitations, Strachey had a final word of warning:

We may leave such people to enjoy their tiny pleasures and comforts: for these will not long remain to them. They will find that in shrinking from the agony of birth they have chosen the agony of death.

It is easy to recognize the form of this argument in, for instance, the quotation from Giles Romilly about the public schools. The Labour Party in politics, the 'progressive' in education, these are the most dangerous because the most insidious enemies. And perhaps the most devastating part of Strachey's argument, as it seemed to the Pragmatists, was that in which he applied these principles to the work of the great liberalizing Edwardian artists. Thus H.G. Wells was seen as 'an ardent disciple of the school of ultra-imperialism: of the world state to be achieved by the coagulation of the capitalist classes of all nations'. Shaw had sacrificed his chance of immortality by eschewing revolutionary activity, and settling instead for 'fame, money, power, and for the enjoyment of these good things in his own lifetime'. *A La Recherche Du Temps Perdu* was an 'odyssey of snobbery', *Ulysses* marked 'the exhaustion of a whole range of possibilities', *The Waste Land* expressed 'the whole agonizing disintegration of an old and once strong social system'. It is interesting to compare Strachey's severity towards such a 'liberal' economist as Keynes ('The next question which Mr Keynes will have to ask himself will be "Am I a Fascist?"'. And the answer will be in the affirmative'), with his tenderness towards such a prophet of violence as Nietzsche. ('It is impossible to achieve the ultimate, though always caustic, revolutionary optimism unless the mind has first been purged of the facile optimism of nineteenth-century liberalism.') *The Coming Struggle For Power* was felt by many to be a deeply shocking book, in its language and its implications. 'That is the way these young men who are raised as gentlemen and given Oxford and Eton training usually turn out,' Lady Mosley said. 'I am sure there is not a single member of the British Union of Fascists who would speak to him today if he met him on the street.'

It is not important to argue whether Strachey's analysis was in absolute terms 'right' or 'wrong' (to Strachey himself in his later days, when he had become a Labour Cabinet Minister, much of it certainly seemed 'wrong'): the significant thing is that for many people what he said seemed to correspond very well with the realities that they saw and sensed around them. Social analysts imagine that they are seeing permanent truths, but really their vision is bounded by the horizon of the next five years, for technological and scientific advances have come so swiftly in this century that most long-term predictions are falsified within a decade by scientific changes which affect the basic social structure. Looking round at the world, seeing the utter inability of the British and American Governments to lessen greatly the number of unemployed, coming into contact with actual human want and misery, many people were inclined to accept the idea of an inevitable struggle for power. Not all, or even the majority, of them received this idea through Strachey's book: just as Strachey's thesis is popularized Marx, so there were writers who further simplified Strachey, or adapted some of his ideas, so that the book's effect was felt by people to whom Strachey was no more than a name. This effect was not, in any case, to make people join the Communist Party – the membership of the Party during the Thirties was smaller than it is today. Rather, *The Coming Struggle For Power* helped to create a whole climate of opinion, a climate in which certain assumptions were almost automatic. It was assumed, for example, that there was some inherent virtue in the working class, a virtue quite independent of the ignorance and prejudice shown by its individual members. It was assumed that the intentions of the Soviet Union were always good, however unfortunately they might be manifested. Censorship in the Soviet Union was not really censorship, imprisonment was essentially a social corrective. These were the feelings, not simply of hardened Party members, nor merely of the Artists and Pragmatists who were delighted to receive this ready-made guide to a philosophy of action, but also of many among the Audience at the base of the pyramid, who found themselves emotionally compelled to believe in the virtue of the Soviet Union as the viciousness of German Fascism became apparent.

The psychological effects of this adherence to a vaguely-held idea of collective action are interesting. As individuals the members of the Audience were still tender-minded, but as a group they had come to accept violence as a necessity, and even perhaps to desire it. It was a psychological need for the solutions to life that appeared to be offered by violence that prompted many pacifically-minded people to reject pacifism. The general attitude of these people towards Communism was one of regretful sympathy. The future, they agreed with Strachey, belonged to Communism, but they believed strongly that their own infusion of liberal feeling would temper Communist harshness, perhaps even change the nature of Communism in Britain.

Once the importance of achieving collective security, through some means other than the League of Nations, had been understood, every event seemed to reinforce this view. The invasion of Abyssinia by Mussolini's Italy had been preceded by the Italian delegation walking contemptuously out of the League; the attempt to apply economic sanctions failed completely: and to let Mussolini go ahead was felt to involve a sort of complicity in his aggression. He should be stopped, then: and how could he be stopped but by a coalition of progressive groups and parties, in which, quite naturally, the Communist Party – as representative, so to speak, of the Soviet Union – must play a leading part? The liberals who accepted this argument never really understood that participation in such a coalition implied an infinite pliability on their own part, a slow stretching of the liberal conscience. This conscience can be seen growing more and more elastic through the years, so that many who were horrified by the German attacks on Jews in 1933, and deeply shocked by the destruction of Guernica in the Spanish Civil War, felt that the bombing of civilians in the Second World War was sad but necessary, and consoled themselves after Hiroshima and Nagasaki with the thought that the dropping of these atomic bombs had ended the war and so been a means of saving lives. What would the attitude of these people have been towards a massacre committed by the Spanish Republicans, a counter-Guernica? The question is rhetorical: they would have said that such a massacre was impossible, that 'our' troops would not do such a thing. When those on 'our' side killed, the conscience rested in momentary abeyance, as this poem by Bernard Spencer conveys.

> I read of a thousand killed.
> And am glad because the scrounging imperial paw
> Was there so bitten:
> As a man at elections is thrilled
> When the results pour in, and the North goes with him
> And the West breaks in the thaw.
>
> (That fighting was a long way off.)
>
> Forgetting therefore an election
> Being fought with votes and lies and catch-cries
> And orator's frowns and flowers and posters' noise,
> Is paid for with cheques and toys:
> Wars the most glorious
> Victory-winged and steeple-uproarious
> ...With the lives, burned-off,
> Of young men and boys.

Slowly, almost imperceptibly, liberals found themselves acknowledging simultaneously pleasure in reading of a thousand dead and sorrow that war meant burned-off lives; swiftly and delicately they touched violence to see if it burned, as a child puts a finger through the flame. In their adherence to collective security there was a masochistic feeling for violence, a longing for immersion in the virtuous strength of the Soviet Union, a desire to identify goodness with success. It was not until the end of the Spanish Civil War that the dreamers drew back, distressed by the discovery that the finger held too long in the flame actually burned.

6

The Heart of a Dream

The year 1936 was not only the middle of a decade, but also the heart of the Thirties dream. Consider: in this year the Left Book Club was founded, the Spanish Civil War began, the Surrealist Exhibition was held, the Jarrow Crusade took place, the first issue of *New Writing* appeared. Fascism in Britain became strongly arrogant and obtrusive. The movement towards collective action, towards a Popular Front, was suddenly no longer the quirk of the political Left but a potent force, adhered to by people of all parties and many beliefs.

There was a political dream, in which Fascism would be checked abroad and at home, and the National Government in Britain thrown out, by a great concerted movement for democratic action supported by all men and women of goodwill. There was an aesthetic dream in which art would be appreciated by the masses, yet produced at a high level of sensibility. The political and aesthetic dreams somehow blended together, so that the sectarian Communist was to lie down with the unpolitical aesthete (at no other time in this century could such an artist as Virginia Woolf have written in the *Daily Worker*), the working-class Socialist to bed with the middle-class Surrealist, and all were to join together in a European movement whose triumph was historically inevitable. It is easy now to see that most of those involved were unprepared to do more than attend a meeting or two and wait for that historically inevitable success to come about, easy to see that they were deceived: yet behind the movement at this time were the most generous impulses of humanity, impulses more valuable by far than the barren knowingness of recent years. It is better to be waiting for Lefty than to be waiting for Godot.

Let us look at two of the events that helped to solidify opinion in support of the Popular Front: the increasing violence of British Fascism and the march from Jarrow.

The Fascists in 1936 felt strong enough, not as a British party but as part of a rapidly growing European movement, to provoke violence by organized marches through the East End. The Liberal MP Sir Percy Harris described their technique.

A large van, looking like a police van, which in itself is irritating, arrives on the scene with a spotlight, and in due course there marches on the scene the military organization of the Blackshirts. The next thing that happens is that a body of police arrives. There is a feeling going right through the East End that somehow or other the police are acting in collusion with the Fascists.

Certainly the police force, never notably sympathetic towards Left-wing movements, seemed always to assume very readily the task of protecting the Fascists from opposition. Early in October the Fascists planned a march which was to begin at the Royal Mint and go through Whitechapel. Long before the march was timed to start, the streets round the Royal Mint were crowded. The police cordoned them off and made way for the Fascists, who came up for the most part in closed vans. More than a dozen wireless vans were used in an attempt to control the crowd, and two airplanes made reconnaissances above the scene. In an attempt to clear a way for the march the police made baton charges in Cable Street, where the crowd had torn up the paving stones and built barricades. There was hand-to-hand fighting between police and demonstrators. Many demonstrators were arrested. The march had been timed to start at half past two, but Mosley did not arrive until a quarter to three. Immediately on his arrival a forest of Union Jacks on decorated poles rose into the air. More unsuccessful attempts were made to disperse the crowd, and when another hour had passed the projected march through White-chapel was called off. Instead the Fascists marched, heavily escorted by police all the way, westwards to the Embankment and thence to Trafalgar Square. Some carried small sticky-back labels saying 'Every Jew is a burden on the back of a Gentile' and 'Kill the dirty Jews', which they affixed to walls and hoardings. On the following Sunday there was a march by anti-Fascists through the East End, which did not need the benefit of police protection. The Fascists made little attempt to interfere with the march, but retaliated by breaking the windows of shops in the Mile End Road with Jewish names on their boards.

There were complaints, not only of police brutality towards anti-

Fascists, but also of the Fascists' own behaviour. 'Sir Oswald's splendid young men fight with their bare fists,' said the veteran author of *Bengal Lancer*, Major Yeats-Brown, in a letter expressing regret that he could not be one of them, but those attacked with razors and knuckledusters, and forced to drink castor oil, told a different story. Interrupters at Fascist meetings were dragged out, kicked in the testicles and brutally beaten. Such meetings as that held at the Albert Hall had, as *The Times* noted, a theatrically military air.

Inside the hall the appearance of Sir Oswald Mosley was preceded by the arrival of lines of Blackshirts, who took up positions in the main aisle, the beating of drums and the sounding of bugles. As Sir Oswald Mosley walked the entire length of the hall to the platform, the Blackshirts and the audience rose and gave the Fascist salute, martial music was played, spot lights shone on Sir Oswald from the galleries, and there was loud cheering.

At this meeting also the Albert Hall was guarded by what some newspapers called, no doubt exaggeratedly, thousands of police: there were enough, anyway, to pack the entire front of the building and to cordon off the rear. A huge crowd milled about outside, and the police smuggled late-arriving Fascists into the hall. Later, said a stop press item in the *Daily Worker*:

Mounted police, now attempting to drive a crowd of 3,000 down Exhibition Road, and meeting with much difficulty owing to the fact that the horses have to tread in and out of traffic, which is at a standstill for half a mile in every direction.

Again many demonstrators were arrested, again there were accusations of police brutality, and of their partiality towards the Fascists. Many people believed these accusations.

In Middlesbrough I had thought that I had known what poverty could mean. But in that town some industry was going on, some people had work. Compared to Jarrow, things on Tees-side were moving. Jarrow in that year, 1932-3, was utterly stagnant. There was no work. No one had a job, except a few railwaymen, officials, the workers in the co-operative Stores, and the few clerks and craftsmen who went out of the town to their jobs each day. The unemployment rate was over 80 per cent.

So Ellen Wilkinson, then Labour candidate and later Member of Parliament for Jarrow. In 1934 she took three hundred people from the constituency to see Ramsay MacDonald, then Prime Minister of the National Government, who was visiting his constituency of Seaham. MacDonald had refused to meet a deputation of Tyneside MPs, but he saw Ellen Wilkinson and eight of the three hundred who had walked nine miles in a gale. He promised special consideration, asked for a written report, said Jarrow would be kept in his mind. As the deputation rose to leave he put his hand on Ellen Wilkinson's shoulder and said: 'Ellen, why don't you go out and preach Socialism, which is the only remedy for all this?' Nothing was done, and when another deputation saw Walter Runciman, then President of the Board of Trade, they were told that nothing could be done. The projected Jarrow Steelworks, which would have brought employment to the town, had been stifled by the Iron and Steel Federation, with the Government's approval. 'Jarrow,' Runciman told the deputation, 'must work out its own salvation.'

This was the background of the march from Jarrow to London which was called the Jarrow Crusade. Runciman's remark caused great indignation, not only in Jarrow, and in July it was suggested that the unemployed men of Jarrow should march to London, telling people on the way of the treatment they had received. The march was sanctioned by the Town Council, and was supported by the whole of Tyneside. About £800 had been raised by an appeal, of which £1 per head was kept for the return journey by train. With the rest of the money the Crusade Committee bought leather and nails for the two hundred men chosen, so that they could mend their own boots. They also bought waterproof groundsheets that could be used as capes. Field kitchen equipment was lent by the Boy Scouts, and a secondhand bus was bought to carry the men's kit and blankets. Prayers were said in every church and chapel in Jarrow, and on 4 October (the day of the Fascist attempt to march through Whitechapel) the march began. A brass band played the crusaders out of the borough boundary. They slept that night in the Church Institute at Chester-le-Street.

According to Ellen Wilkinson the Jarrow Communist Party had no more than seven members, and only two of these were on the march. Whether or not these figures are exactly true, it is certain that the Jarrow Crusade was not Communist-inspired: certain also that there was a great deal of Communist inspiration behind some of the ten other groups of marchers who were converging on London from various parts of Britain, to protest against the Means Test. The adroitness with which the Communists stressed their own part in the marches, and the enthusiasm of their comparatively few participants, made it possible for some Church dignitaries and Members of Parliament to accuse the marchers of an attempt to exert 'revolutionary mob pressure', although in fact they were wholly law-abiding.

In most places they were warmly received. People cheered as they passed, and gave them money and food. Considerable crowds came and listened attentively at their evening meetings. In many towns both Conservative and Labour parties made arrangements for their reception. Ellen Wilkinson wrote of the difference made by the kind of reception they got.

> Sometimes we came in from the dark road to beautifully set tables, napery and crockery and bright lights. Immediately the men smartened up.... But in those towns, mercifully few, where the tables were bare boards, and tea was poured from buckets into our own mugs, the men who had appeared so smart and alert at the well-set tables, suddenly looked 'poor-law', and just as grubby as their angry MP.

Just occasionally they met with hostility. One north-eastern contingent found a police cordon barring the way from Thirsk to York. They were not allowed to march through York as they had intended, but stayed at a workhouse where they were given only bread and margarine to eat, and where two hundred police kept a watch on them. But this was exceptional. Almost everywhere else the authorities were friendly.

The march from Jarrow to London took a little more than a month. After the men had been on the road for a week the Cabinet issued a statement, saying that such marches were wholly undesirable, and that they would not receive a deputation. The TUC and the Labour Party Executive also frowned on the marches. A group of doctors and medical students looked after the Jarrow men, and improvised a clinic each evening in a corner of the chapel or drill hall where they slept. 'What a blessing this medical care was,' Ellen Wilkinson wrote,

'I only understood to the full when, the Jarrow men having returned home, I went to help the men who had marched from Durham without such skilled assistance. I had to cut socks that had become embedded in broken blisters, and bandage the feet of men who must have walked in agony.' The march was, indeed, a severe strain on men who had for years been under-nourished and badly fed.

The mass meeting which assembled in Hyde Park to greet the marchers was organized by the Communist Party, although the Labour Party's leader, Clement Attlee, was among the speakers. Thousands of people greeted them, banners waved, songs were sung: but when the cheering died, the actual results of the great march were seen to be rather meagre. The presentation of the Jarrow petition, as Ellen Wilkinson says, could only be a gesture; the pleasure of giving an uncomfortable hour to the Minister of Labour, Ernest Brown, as he listened to the marchers' pleas, was another gesture. Jarrow got a certain amount of help from the new tube works sponsored by Sir John Jarvis, but beyond that was the icy indifference of Runciman, which was also the indifference of the Government. The protest marches, as Ellen Wilkinson put it, 'told the world', and in a practical sense they could do nothing more.

Marches, counter-marches, petitions, crusades: these things seemed to make it inevitable that sides should be taken, and how could the Audience possibly be on any side but that of the Crusaders, the democrats? It was a realization of the change in British intellectual life, a change that was pushing the Audience slowly towards sympathy with all Left-wing ideas and movements, that prompted the foundation of John Lehmann's *New Writing* in April 1936. The poets need no longer talk revolution to an empty room. Let them talk not of revolution but of gradual necessary change, and they would find many listeners.

In form, *New Writing* was a book rather than a periodical, and its brief manifesto included a paragraph expressing its unpolitical nature in a typically political way.

New Writing will appear twice yearly, and will be devoted to imaginative writing, mainly of young authors. It does not intend to concern itself with literary theory, or the criticism of contemporaries....*New Writing* is first and foremost interested in literature, and though it does not intend to open its pages to writers of reactionary or Fascist sentiments, it is independent of any political party.

The primary function of *New Writing* was to provide a bigger audience for writers of the Auden Group. Here the prose writers could be seen at full stretch, and the delicate, sad, gently ironic talent revealed in Christopher Isherwood's Berlin stories delighted thousands of people who had previously been irritated by the theatrical work of Auden and Isherwood. These stories expressed feelings about Germany, Jews, life itself, that were recognizable and sympathetic; there was nothing flippant or violent about them, they were faithful evocations of a vanished way of thought and feeling that, whatever its limitations, seemed admirable in contrast to the Fascism that had wiped it away. And the Auden Group did not now appear, as they had done in earlier collections, as isolated and slightly eccentric figures. Lehmann printed many pieces by writers in other countries who were in sympathy with the Popular Front line – the first three issues included more than twenty stories and poems by French, Russian, German, Italian and Chinese writers, several of them (not the Russians) living in exile. The work of Auden, too, now appealed to the wide public that enjoyed *New Writing*. His poetry appeared greatly broadened, or as some thought softened, in the collection, *Look, Stranger*, which came out in October 1936. In Auden's vision of the changed and changing world there was now little of that early aggressive scoutmaster's or commissar's tone. Instead he magnificently expressed in his own person what the Audience collectively felt about their historical mission and final fate.

> And now no path on which we move
> But shows already traces of
>   Intentions not our own,
> Thoroughly able to achieve
> What our excitement could conceive,
>   But our hearts left alone.
>
> For what by nature and by training
> We loved, has little strength remaining:
>   Though we would gladly give
> The Oxford colleges, Big Ben,
> And all the birds in Wicken Fen,
>   It has no wish to live.

Soon through the dykes of our content
The crumpling flood will force a rent,
    And, taller than a tree,
Hold sudden death before our eyes
Whose river dreams long hid the size
    And vigours of the sea.

The sympathetic nature of what Auden was saying here (we are
defeated, yes, but we are still the nicest people) was accompanied by
an increased flexibility in the verse. Some of the poems in this book
talk about revolution, but they are not in their form or their content
at all revolutionary. His sales increased very considerably. *Look,
Stranger* was published in a first edition of 2,350 copies, and within
three months a reprint of 2,000 copies was called for. These may not
seem to be large sales, but they were quite remarkably high figures
for the time. A year later the seal was set on his popularity by the
award to him of the King's Gold Medal for poetry. The presentation
was made at Buckingham Palace. Auden said afterwards,

> The whole ceremony took only three minutes, and there were
> only three people present. The Poet Laureate presented me to the
> King, and the King presented me with the medal. I couldn't tell
> you a thing that was said, or a thing that I saw.

Nowadays poets accept honours (when they are offered) as a matter
of course, and any surprise one feels is limited to the fact that the
Royal Medal was offered to an unconventional Left-wing poet. At
the time, though, Auden's acceptance of the Medal was a shock to
many of his admirers. It seemed, like so many things then, to have
a symbolic importance; acceptance of the Royal Medal looked like a
betrayal of Auden's own poetical and political beliefs. Geoffrey Grigson's comment reflects the uneasiness of other poets in a way that
now seems slightly comic.

> There are many possible explanations. We do not know the
> right one. If it is one of the hostile explanations which do Mr
> Auden no credit, – well, Balzac was not always as good as his
> novels or Dryden as good as his poems. It may be true that the
> joke is much more on the medal than it is on Auden. Anyone who
> knows Auden will realize that, but there is no good reason for
> taking the Royal Medal, all the same.

Such feelings were confined to Artists and Pragmatists. Among the Audience, Auden's acceptance of the Royal Medal did him no harm at all.

Many of the prose contributions to these early issues of *New Writings* showed the old desire to view life in terms of school.

> Ever since breakfast the tutor had been preparing to tell Mr Parkinson that he would rather not accompany him and the boy to the races. 'Why should I?' he thought. 'I may have been forced to sell myself as a purveyor of the kind of trash that's required for a public school Common Entrance examination, but I'm not going to act as a footman as well.'

This was the opening of an 'episode from the unique work, half novel, half allegory, now being written by Edward Upward', a work in which there was a 'deep current of philosophical and social criticism beneath the fantasy'. Readers outside the particular literary swim in which the name of Upward was bracketed with those of Auden, Spender and Isherwood, were unable to understand this deeply respectful treatment of a writer who had not published a book. When *Journey to the Border* finally appeared, it was seen to be a fantasy with the tang of Mortmere about it, a work of the most serious and indeed solemn implications which was at the same time a bit of a joke.

As balance for these solemn jokes, John Lehmann introduced into *New Writing* what may best be called a line of documentary propaganda. Pieces of this kind in early numbers included a sketch of a blackleg's activities in a railway strike, another about feeling hungry, another about a foreman boss, another about working class Jewish family life in Whitechapel, another of the first hunger march in 1922, another of a coal miner's life. These stories and documents were competently written, yet in their careful avoidance of rhetoric they offered in the end little more than a documentation of objects and occupations.

> Jack Davies worked with a swiftness that showed how used he was to the semi-darkness. He allowed the coil of yellow fuse to slip through his hand until it was three inches less than the length of the broom handle; then cut the fuse with a sharp jab of the knife against the handle.
>
> 'That'll be about four feet six,' he spoke aloud to the darkness.

'Aye, it'll do all right. There'll be three inches outside of the bore-
hole, and three pills 'ull knock it quite hard enough – surely.'

It seems extraordinary that there can ever have been a time when
this sort of writing appeared anything but extremely dull, but to
many of the intelligentsia it seemed that at last the working class was
finding its literary voice. About the recognition of this voice there
was a good deal of condescension, of Doctor Johnson's feeling about
the dog walking upon his hind legs. How splendid it was that they
were able to write at all! It would have been too much to expect that
they should produce anything interesting in the way of art, but what
a lot of enviable experience they had to draw on....

I was arguing the other day with a friend who insisted that there is
something funny in Tom Lehrer's songs about all of us frying together
or baking together or being in other ways incinerated together when
the H-bomb drops. My friend, a keen nuclear disarmer, was briskly
dismissive. 'If you don't think they're funny, that's all there is to it.'
The subject matter was irrelevant. But wasn't there some conceivable
point, I asked, at which the subject matter might affect appreciation
of the humour? Supposing that, instead of singing about our total
extinction by nuclear bomb or about the pleasures of masochism,
Tom Lehrer sang about piling up the corpses in concentration camps
or about always being able to tell a Yid by the length of his nose or
about the pleasure of using your whip on an African – and sang about
these things, of course, in his own particular neutral way – could
such songs possibly be funny? It was difficult to imagine it, he said,
but yes, they could. In principle at least, anything could be funny.

Our argument abruptly ended, as the other side of the Tom Lehrer
record was put on: it left me dismally conscious of a gap in feeling
between the generations. My friend was seventeen years old when
the war began. He missed altogether the moral attitude that stamped
those of us who came to maturity in the Thirties and that, whatever
we may think to the contrary, has never really been extinguished in
our minds. It seems to me still that to be prepared to laugh at your
own beliefs is the mark of a mind not broad but shallow. I would not
expect a Christian to be convulsed with laughter by witty blasphemies
about religion, or a Communist to find anything funny in a song
ascribing all Lenin's activities to his Oedipus complex, or an extreme

British nationalist to be amused by an obscene song about the Union Jack: nor, for that matter, would I expect anybody who had been moved by great works of art to find uproariously comic a song that described their destruction with the utmost relish. Those who feel deeply, who believe intensely, have never been prepared to laugh about their beliefs and feelings.

This is a circuitous way of saying that at the heart of the Thirties dream there was a conception of social morality. A painting, a play, a novel, even a lyric, is first of all a social event: a remark that became a cliché in the Thirties, but is almost revolutionary again today. It does not exist (we went on to say) as something pure and absolute, a thing in itself, and cannot be considered apart from the society in which it was created. It follows that the first approach to a work of art must always be a social one: the fact that Evelyn Waugh is a reactionary writer, for instance, affects the style and content of his humour, and imposes certain limitations on his art. We can understand him best by tracing the steps through which he has become in essence a spokesman of British Imperialism....

I am parodying, but only a little, as those who remember a brilliant wartime article by Nigel Dennis on 'Evelyn Waugh and the Churchillian Renaissance' will know: and it seems to me still that this social approach, which shouldn't exclude complementary textual and biographical and aesthetic approaches, has produced much of the best criticism of our time. That it was responsible for some extreme crudities also is undeniable, and it can't be denied, either, that about our faithfulness to social criticism there was sometimes a strong flavour of absurdity. I remember very well a long discussion, indeed an endless discussion, in which I was involved, on the question: are the Marx Brothers social satirists? Nobody denied that their films were funny, but one faction maintained that they were simply clowns and gagsters of genius, while another believed that their films were unconscious Anarchist criticisms of society, and a third thought that Groucho and Chico were doing more than cocking a snook at respectability, regarded *Duck Soup* as an anti-militarist comedy, and believed that Hollywood producers had felt it necessary to introduce an orthodox 'story line' because the social criticism in the early Marx Brothers films was too savage. For these purists (I was one of them) only *Animal Crackers, Monkey Business, Horsefeathers* and *Duck Soup* were admissible within the strict limits of social satire on the screen....

'I flatter myself,' the bore says, showing all his false teeth in a terrible grin, 'I flatter myself, gentlemen, that I have a pretty good sense of humour.' He does indeed: yet if the seriousness of the Thirties was of a kind that today seems intolerably pompous, the comedy had a gaiety that was wholly individual. Consider a few quotations side by side.

Dear Bill,
Did you read the new Soviet Constitution? If you did, you'll know that Georgia has now been made an independent republic on an equal footing with any other republic in the Soviet Union.
It was the Five-Year Plan, in Georgia as everywhere else, that did the trick. The Five-Year Plan produced the machines, and the machines made collectivization possible....

In the face of the 1607 rebellion of the Diggers, how can he maintain hope and trust in humanist values? Money has conquered.... Is it to be thought that Shakespeare, the devoted Warwickshire man, the author of *Lear*, would have followed the fortunes of the rebellious Diggers unmoved? His heart was wrung, and yet he felt more strongly than ever the fact that the people were politically immature, unable to help themselves by insurrection. What else, at that time and place, was left to him but the anarchist fury of Timon?

Once as I sat in a snack bar
I talked to a young man,
He had a hammer and sickle badge
And a bandaged hand,
I asked him how he was injured,
Was it in some street fight?
He turned to the pin-table,
And said, We ask for Life.

It would be difficult to find anything much worse in their different ways than these extracts from *Left Review*. Bill can hardly be blamed if he abandoned John Lehmann's long 'Letter From Tiflis' after those opening lines; it is hard to believe that Jack Lindsay's analysis of Shakespeare is anything but a parody; Maurice Carpenter's poem is a perfect demonstration in the art of sinking. The Soviet Union and

Shakespeare, these were subjects about which jokes were simply not permissible; but on the other side of this utter seriousness was anarchic comedy.

> Miss Twye was soaping her breasts in the bath
> When she heard behind her a meaning laugh
> And to her amazement she discovered
> A wicked man in the bathroom cupboard.

> Captain Busby had put his beard in his mouth and sucked it, then took it out and spat on it then put it in and sucked it then walked on down the street thinking hard.
> Suddenly he put his wedding ring in his trilby hat and put the hat on a passing kitten. Then he carefully calculated the width of the pavement with a pair of adjustable sugar-tongs. This done he knitted his brows. Then he walked on thinking hard.

Gavin Ewart's verse about Miss Twye, Philip O'Connor's curiously memorable nonsense about Captain Busby, show Thirties comedy at its most deliberately irresponsible. Certainly there was no single *tone* of writing in the Thirties, as a single tone, with only slight variations, is sounded by the early work of John Osborne, John Braine, Kingsley Amis, Arnold Wesker. It is possible to take a quite different view of the Thirties from that which sees the period as one of breast-beating earnestness, and to maintain that it is marked by an excessive regard for the trivial and the flippant. The solemnity associated at this time with Cambridge was attacked by Auden on several occasions, and by Gavin Ewart in a poem which begins with the line, 'Imagine all the dons in the attitude of buggers.'

The key to this, as to so much else, was provided by Auden when he said in an essay on psychology and art that 'There must always be two kinds of art, escape-art, for man needs escape as he needs food and deep sleep, and parable-art, that art which shall teach man to unlearn hatred and learn love.' This remark was used as a justification of much that Auden perhaps did not intend, but it is certainly true in the sense that the dream of the Thirties comprehended both earnestness and irresponsibility. I suppose this safety valve of humour, as it was expressed for example in Louis MacNeice's 'Bagpipe Music', was a sort of nihilism.

It's no go the merrygoround, it's no go the rickshaw,
All we want is a limousine and a ticket for the peepshow.
Their knickers are made of crêpe-de-chine, their shoes are made
    of python,
Their halls are lined with tiger rugs and their wall with heads of bison.

John MacDonald found a corpse, put it under the sofa,
Waited till it came to life and hit it with a poker,
Sold its eyes for souvenirs, sold its blood for whisky,
Kept its bones for dumb-bells to use when he was fifty.

It's no go the Yogi-Man, it's no go Blavatsky,
All we want is a bank balance and a bit of skirt in a taxi.

Annie MacDougall went to milk, caught her foot in the heather,
Woke to hear a dance record playing of Old Vienna.
It's no go your maidenheads, it's no go your culture,
All we want is a Dunlop tyre and the devil mend the puncture.

The Laird o' Phelps spent Hogmanay declaring he was sober,
Counted his feet to prove the fact and found he had one foot over.
Mrs Carmichael had her fifth, looked at the job with repulsion,
Said to the midwife 'Take it away; I'm through with over-
    production.'

It's no go the gossip column, it's no go the Ceilidh,
All we want is a mother's help and a sugar-stick for the baby.

Willie Murray cut his thumb, couldn't count the damage,
Took the hide of an Ayrshire cow and used it for a bandage.
His brother caught three hundred cran when the seas were lavish,
Threw the bleeders back in the sea and went upon the parish.

It's no go the Herring Board, it's no go the Bible,
All we want is a packet of fags when our hands are idle.

It's no go the picture palace, it's no go the stadium,
It's no go the country cot with a pot of pink geraniums.
It's no go the Government grants, it's no go the elections,
Sit on your arse for fifty years and hang your hat on a pension.

It's no go my honey love, it's no go my poppet;
Work your hands from day to day, the winds will blow the profit.
The glass is falling hour by hour, the glass will fall for ever,
But if you break the bloody glass you won't hold up the weather.

It may be true that in the end the attempt to blend parable-art and escape-art is a sort of schizophrenia, doing severe mental damage. The desire to do so, and the belief that it could be done, was an integral part of the Thirties dream, as it evolved in the little magazines, the Group Theatre, the Left Book Club, Surrealism.

7

The Little Magazines

New Verse, then, has a clear function,...It favours only its time, belonging to no literary or politico-literary cabal, cherishing bombs only for masqueraders and for the everlasting 'critical' rearguard of nastiness, now represented so ably and variously by the *Best Poems of the Year*, the Book Society and all the gang of big shot reviewers.

New Verse No. 1, January 1933

A writer's usefulness depends on his influence: that is to say, on the size and enthusiasm of his public: or, in the case of writers' writers, on his ability to set scores of other pens working.

Left Review No. 2, November 1934

New Verse and *Left Review* represent the aesthetic impulses of the period in their most extreme form. No other editor of the decade was so sharply intelligent as Geoffrey Grigson. The poems that appeared in *New Verse* passed through the sieve of a mind deeply distrustful of all generalizations that led away from the particular, of all poems constructed out of rhetorical feeling rather than out of direct observation. It was a logical consequence of this attitude to condemn the 'nauseating concern for *poetry*' which Grigson found in Michael Roberts's introduction to the *Faber Book of Modern Verse*. 'Poetry (if you like, these are overstatements for the point) is of no interest except for poets. Anthologies are of no interest except to readers. Readers should be interested in *poems* only, not in the category or in developments'; and, admitting that there was no better anthology of modern verse on the same scale, he would go no further in praise of its compiler than to say that 'Michael the Mountaineer is not the biggest blockhead in the anthology trade'. This might, indeed, in *New Verse* almost pass for praise: for those poets who gave the wrong response when their feelings or language were tested with the Grigson inflation-counter, were relentlessly treated. 'Why has anyone published, does anyone praise, does anyone read, the verse of Mr George Barker? Mr Barker's libidinous development has been upset. He is turned in on himself in

a morbid narcissism, loving himself, and anxious to be loved, in order
to preserve his own self-importance. It may be excellent that Mr
Barker should be healing himself in prose-poems, but he should do
it by himself on the other side of the house...Mr Swingler observes
only the obvious. So does Mr Pudney, but he is more able to express
it. He borrows more like an artist, but uses what he borrows and
what he provides insipidly. His poems possess a character but one
like stale water....He (Rayner Heppenstall) is a sluggish bore, a
Hopkins-Binyon bore, a tangle of pimpled laurels bore, a costive
bore, a really I do not know Sir James Frazer bore; always absolutely
a BORE. He is also a yearning, blind, deaf, word-gargling, 1930
book-bedded, prose-sniping, egg-bound bore, a bore pretending to
purpose, a culture bore.' The work of all these poets had appeared
in early numbers of *New Verse*, and to those who find nothing but
deliberate and objectionable rudeness in these reviews it will seem
astonishing that Barker's work appeared there again, after the review
of his *Poems* headed 'Nertz'. In part this may be explained by the
fact that the influence of *New Verse* was very great, within its narrow
area: in part by an unspecific feeling, even among some of the poets
castigated, that Grigson was doing something useful. His choice of
poems showed by omission the kind of thing to be avoided, and this
is almost the most valuable thing a young poet can learn in any
period. Reading again the complete file of *New Verse* for the six years
of its life one finds no poems written in truly dead Georgian language,
comparatively few that are pretentiously obscure, a good many (this
was the chief weakness of *New Verse*, as of Auden) that are trivial:

> While the Persians
> Undoubtedly were given to
> Several interesting perversions
> I consider
> The political customs of England
> Were, in growth, far rapider.
>
> Gavin Ewart

But I suppose the triviality should be seen in the light of the problem
most keenly felt by poets at this time: when I think of human suffering,
Fascism, unemployment, the prospect of war, how can I go on writing
poetry at all? In the face of such a problem the deliberately trivial,
the comically obscure, the outrageously nonsensical, often seems an
answer, as the deliberate rejection of logic in much recent writing is

in a sense a defiant disregard of the threat implied by the atomic bomb. *New Verse* set a standard rather than a style, yet there was a certain poetic style, based on careful observation and deliberately elegant choice of epithet, associated with its younger contributors: a style labelled by its opponents bourgeois objectivism. What else, the editors of *Left Review* may have asked themselves, could be said about a periodical that proclaimed itself 'neither True Blue nor Red, nor Liberal, a dull confusion of all colours, believing that the extent of a political situation is strict and near and mean compared with the immensely far-off limit of every rich individuality that needs to be explored on behalf of all individuals'?

If one imagines the 'Auden Group' not as several individuals but as one many-headed monster, the split in this monster's personality is nakedly shown in the paths taken by these two magazines, with Auden moving over to the humanist unpolitical *New Verse* side, Day Lewis plumping emphatically for the Communist *Left Review*, Spender wavering lyrically between, and all the little Audens, Day Lewises and Spenders taking up their appropriate poetical-political positions. The editorial attitude of *Left Review* is made clear in the quotation above. You are either with us or against us: and if you are with us, you will recognize that the principal function of writers today is to 'use their pens and their influence against imperialist war and in defence of the Soviet Union.' So Day Lewis's poem, 'The Road These Times Must Take', in the second issue, began:

> Yes, why do we all, seeing a communist, feel small? That small
> Catspaw ruffles our calm

and ends:

> Mark him, workers, and all who wish the world aright –
> He is what your sons will be, the road these times must take.

A poem by Tom Wintringham answered him, in a style that might be a gruesome parody of Day Lewis's own earlier manner:

> Marx for your map, Lenin's theodolite –
> This is a thing Smolny's October showed –
> Crag-contour pioneered, valley and peak's height
> Known: all is ready? No, steel wire must be
> Inseparable from concrete, you from me.

The chief criticism to be made of *Left Review* is that the effect of its conscious party line was to make its contributors write so uncommonly badly. In 'Electricity Comes to Husler Street', for instance, old Mr Myers finds this new-fangled electricity is wonderful, but simply hasn't enough shillings for the meter. He goes back sadly to dimness and a pennyworth of candles. A group of young people come down the street selling *Russia Today*, and give him a copy. His eye falls on the headline: Electrification *plus Soviet Power* equals Socialism. 'He began muttering, meditatively, as he sat down to read.'

In case it should be thought that this is exceptionally crude propaganda, here are the titles of some other prose pieces: 'Monday Morning in the Machine Shop', 'The Late Duty Porter', 'Soap and Clothes', 'Young Worker', 'Overtime on Aero Engines', 'Clerks, Wanted'. The paper's editors – at first Montagu Slater, Amabel Williams-Ellis and Tom Wintringham, later Edgell Rickword and Randall Swingler – did not lack sensibility or talent, but they thought it right that this talent should be fitted into a Communist pattern. 'It is the strongest argument for a Writer's International,' Slater remarked, 'that it can bring writers into touch with life. "Life", in this context, equals the class struggle.' They abdicated from their responsibilities as editors in the sense that their chief concern was not to raise the level of writing among their working-class contributors but to extirpate the heresies found among the bourgeois writers of talent who were sympathetic to Communism. We have learned now that writers cannot artificially transform themselves in this way, that social criticism must proceed from the knowledge and limitations of an individual personality, and not from the attempt of that individual to adapt himself to the standpoint of an ideal state. In the Thirties writers, or some writers, learned this lesson painfully, and with unhappy results.

The sort of propaganda printed in *Left Review* becomes literature only when it is produced by an artist of genius who feels himself to be part of a revolutionary movement. In England no such movement existed: and the most successful things in the magazine were the satirical drawings produced each month by James Boswell, James Fitton and others. It is much easier, no doubt it is, to be satirical about politicians than to show truthfully the wretched lives and narrow horizons of the poor or to depict lyrically the advance of the masses, but the level at which the paper's black and white artists worked was a consistently high one.

8

Group and Unity

The Group Theatre was founded in 1932 by Rupert Doone and a dozen friends, among them Auden and the painter Robert Medley, who had been at school with Auden. 'I began writing poetry one Sunday afternoon in 1922 because a friend suggested that I should,' Auden said long afterwards, and the friend was Robert Medley. For three years the Theatre produced work for very small audiences; then, late in 1935, it had a London season at the Westminster Theatre, and for the first time became widely known. A small number of people was responsible for the Group Theatre productions. Rupert Doone, who had been trained in classical ballet and had worked with Diaghilev, directed personally most of the productions; costumes, scenery and masks were done by Robert Medley; and music was composed by Herbert Murrill, William Alwyn and Auden's friend Benjamin Britten. Other people – Tyrone Guthrie, John Piper and Henry Moore among them – worked with the Theatre at times. The influence of Uncle Wiz, as Auden was known among them, brooded over all.

The Group Theatre had aesthetic ideas, and it had a social attitude; the first springing largely from Doone, the second from Auden. 'The form we envisage for our plays is analogous to modern musical comedy, or the premediaeval folk play,' Doone said. He considered that theatrical art was 'an art of the body, presented by living people in action'. The theatre was intended to depict 'a life of action and the senses', and it had lagged behind the life it served. 'New forms are wanted to express the life of today.' He called for the establishment of a permanent company of actors working together, and for auditoriums that would command a complete view from every seat by a turn of the head. And the theatre, he said needed more than this permanent company of actors, it needed 'artists, poets, musicians'.

In a collection of aphorisms printed in the programme for *The Dance of Death*, which was written specially for the Group Theatre, Auden emphasized some of Doone's points.

Drama began as the act of a whole community. Ideally there
would be no spectators. In practice every member of the audience
should feel like an understudy.

Drama is essentially an art of the body. The basis of acting is
acrobatics, dancing, and all forms of physical skill. The music hall,
the Christmas pantomime, and the country house charade are the
most living drama of today.

Drama should not be documentary (that was a province of the
film), it should not analyse character (that was done by the novel).
It should take for its subjects the universally familiar stories of its
own society and generation. 'The audience, like the child listening
to the fairy tale, ought to know what is going to happen next.'

Auden's aphorisms, and most of Doone's remarks, were blueprints
for dramatic art in a society that did not exist. They were partly
realized much later, with some inevitable popularization or vulgari-
zation, in Joan Littlewood's Stratford productions. Even in these,
the gap between what the plays said, and what their audiences
believed, was very wide. The West End production of *The Hostage*
offered a fine comic contrast between the rich ranting rebellious life
upon the stage, obscene and blasphemous, and the well-fed respect-
ably-dressed middle-class audience, which hadn't the slightest wish
to participate in the action. The Group Theatre was never anything
like the act of a whole community. It was a gesture by middle-class
radicals to a middle-class liberal audience.

In part the Group Theatre's limitations sprang, especially in
its first London season, from a deliberate stylization and formality
that slowed down the movement of the plays – *The Dance of Death*,
Sweeney Agonistes, *The Dog Beneath the Skin*, and the rest. The use of
masks and the introduction of fragments of ballet had an effect that
was often the reverse of the spontaneity intended. The Theatre found
much opposition among the dramatic critics of the national newspapers, who had little sympathy with its artistic intentions and none
at all with its social ideas, but it was sharply criticized also by those
on its own side of the fence. 'We should like less prancing and bad
dancing, less complacence, less guidance, and more stiff thinking
combined with spontaneity,' Grigson said, voicing what many others
felt. But the chief reason for the Group Theatre's failure ever to
become more than a fashionable entertainment for the middle-class
intelligentsia lay in the inability of Uncle Wiz, and his collaborator

Christopher Isherwood, ever to be wholly serious about their play writing.

> We present to you this evening a picture of the decline of a class, of how its members dream of a new life, but secretly desire the old, for there is death inside them. We show you that death as a dancer.

The seriousness of these opening words, spoken by the announcer in Auden's *Dance of Death*, is hardly justified by the course of the action, in which the cult of athleticism is mildly mocked, Fascism is parodied, and an attempt is made through death to reach 'the very heart of reality'. All of these attempts to solve social problems through death fail, and at the end Karl Marx appears beaming, with two young communists. The Chorus sings.

> O Mr Marx, you've gathered
> All the material facts
> You know the economic
> Reasons for our acts.

Marx solemnly pronounces: 'The instruments of production have been too much for him. He is liquidated.'

At this time Brecht was little known in Britain, and even as late as 1952 Raymond Williams' *Drama From Ibsen to Eliot* managed to leave Brecht unmentioned. The immense debt owed by the Auden and Isherwood plays to Brecht was not realized, but many who saw the plays felt uneasily that serious social comment could not be made to a mass audience in these flippant terms. Yet the boldness involved in abandoning the standard three act play, and in turning jokes and music hall songs to theatrical use, seemed at the time dazzlingly new. *The Dog Beneath the Skin* was certainly enormously enjoyable. The magnificence of Auden's choruses, spoken by Veronica Turleigh and Gyles Isham, made one feel that any way of getting such verse spoken on stage was desirable:

> Now through night's caressing grip
> Earth and all her oceans slip.
> Capes of China slide away
> From her fingers into day,

And the Americas incline
Coasts towards her shadow line.
Now the ragged vagrants creep
Into crooked holes to sleep:
Just and unjust, worst and best,
Change their places as they rest:
Awkward lovers lie in fields
Where disdainful beauty yields:
While the splendid and the proud
Naked stand before the crowd
And the losing gambler gains
And the beggar entertains.

But the picture of life and humanity created in the choruses was one thing, and the action of the play quite another.

Men will profess devotion to almost anything; to God, to Humanity, to Truth, to Beauty: but their first thought on meeting is: 'Beware!'

They put their trust in Reason or the Feelings of the Blood, but they will not trust a stranger with half-a-crown.

Beware of those with no obvious vices; of the chaste, the non-smoker and drinker, the vegetarian:

Beware of those who show no inclination towards making money: there are even less innocent forms of power.

Beware of yourself:

Have you not heard your own heart whisper: 'I am the nicest person in this room?'

Asking to be introduced to someone 'real': someone unlike all those people over there?

You have wonderful hospitals and a few good schools:

Repent.

The precision of your instruments and the skill of your designers is unparalleled:

Unite.

Your knowledge and your power are capable of infinite extension:

Act.

Such choruses seem part of the parable-art that is to teach us to unlearn hatred and learn love: but much of the rest of the play was escape-art simply. It did not merely employ the *technique* of 'modern musical comedy', it *was* that musical comedy, or something so near to it that the edge of satire was indiscernible. One of the few passages of genuine satire, in which Destructive Desmond spits on and slashes a Rembrandt picture to the applause of the fashionable audience in the Nineveh Hotel, was removed from the stage version. The total effect was that the choruses and the action seemed to belong to different plays. What was all this agreeable nonsense about a man dressed up as a dog (and a long-lost heir too) to do with choruses proclaiming that

Under the local images your blood has conjured,
We show you man caught in the trap of his terror, destroying himself.

The setting of musical comedy and fairy tale was deliberately devised to exemplify Auden's ideas about drama, but in truth Alan and the dog, the General and the Vicar, were not universal symbols but private jokes. *The Dog Beneath the Skin* showed perfectly the schizophrenic nature of Auden and Isherwood as dramatists. It was the most enjoyable of failures – but what a wonderful play it might have been, had the action been conceived with the seriousness of the choruses.

The attempt to find some way of reconciling private jokes and public events was very evident in *The Ascent of F.6* and *On the Frontier*, produced by the theatre at the end of 1938. These plays were technically much more skilful than *The Dog Beneath the Skin*, but they were still marked by that distaste for the 'ordinary people' to whom they nominally spoke, that is so marked a feature of Auden's work. The drama in *The Ascent of F.6* is conceived in psychological terms, and in *On the Frontier* verse has been almost completely subdued to prose. But these gestures towards popularity were not enough. The earlier plays were really a presage of something new – one can see their influence, together with that of Brecht and of the American musical, in the Theatre Workshop productions of the Fifties. The later plays are much more nearly conventional.

For me the Group Theatre was chiefly interesting as an exemplification of the ideas of Uncle Wiz, but one mustn't leave it at that. The ritualistic production of *Sweeney Agonistes*, a fragment of drama that has fructified in many curious ways, was extremely interesting and imaginative, and during the whole of the Thirties the existence of the Group Theatre was a positive incitement towards the production of social drama in verse. The Theatre was hampered by lack of money, but its chief limitation was that imposed by the conceptions of Doone and Auden. The Group Theatre bore much the same relation to Unity Theatre that *New Verse* bore to *Left Review*: that is, its directors and practitioners put aesthetic standards before social ones, although they still wanted to change society. Adherents of the Group Theatre were apt to say that Unity was not so much theatre as it was theatrical propaganda; supporters of Unity retorted that the Group Theatre was not so much artistic as arty. Both criticisms, unhappily, were partly true, but it was true also that Group and Unity embodied the only new ideas of dramatic production in Britain during the decade.

The thing that immediately and obviously distinguishes Unity Theatre from the Group Theatre is that it grew out of a desire to dramatize the struggles of the Labour movement, and not out of a formal interest in theatre: its conceptions were practical, not aesthetic. From mass declamations, sketches, monologues, songs, delivered in public and often in the open air; from Sunday night performances, Left Theatre clubs and Rebel Theatre societies, Unity Theatre emerged. It found a permanent home in 1937, in a building in Camden Town that had been a Methodist Chapel and a doss house. The Chapel was converted into a theatre by trade unionists, who did their jobs of carpentering and engineering for nothing. Most of those who acted in its plays were amateurs, and all of them were unpaid. Some out of work professional actors were paid expenses, and occasionally slept in the theatre.

The prime virtue of such a theatre as Unity is enthusiasm, the kind of enthusiasm that can often transcend inadequacies of acting and production – although some of the productions were highly imaginative, and many good actors began their careers in the Theatre. Its chief limitation was the fact that Unity audiences demanded optimism and political radicalism, and had no patience with subtleties of expression. When the Group Theatre produced Stephen Spender's *Trial of a Judge* at Unity, the regular Unity audience stayed away; and this was not only because seat prices had been put up, but because the whole feeling of the play was antipathetic to them. The Communists were awarded the victory, but as Kenneth Allott said in reviewing the play, 'all the best arguments and all the feeling speeches go into the mouth of the judge', and the judge was a liberal. The Unity Theatre audience wanted to see plays about the kind of social struggles·they could understand. Few things interested them less than an abstract argument about justice in the mind of a judge.

The ideal conception behind Unity Theatre was not far removed from Auden's aphorisms. Drama as an act of the community; no spectators, only participants; characters simplified, easily recognizable and over lifesize; the subject general and universal: these ideas came much nearer to fulfilment in Unity's *Waiting for Lefty*, by the American radical playwright, Clifford Odets, than in any Group Theatre production. Since *Waiting For Lefty*, the most famous piece of Left Wing theatre in the Thirties, is now practically unperformed, it may be interesting to look at the play again.

The performance takes place on a bare stage, occupied by six or seven seated men. They are a committee of workers, and they are listening to Harry Fatt, the official trade unionist, who is urging us not to strike. Us: for we, the audience, are the union members Fatt is speaking to, we are part of the play. Several members of the cast planted in the audience interrupt Fatt as he talks. A union goon, a gunman, lolls against the proscenium.

Fatt urges us not to strike. The top man of the country (that is, Roosevelt) is looking after our interests. 'The man in the White House is the one I'm referrin' to. That's why the times ain't ripe for a strike. He's working day and night....' Voices in the audience ask, 'Where is Lefty?' Fatt is indignant, the gunman looks grave. Several members of the Committee tell their stories – a white spot picks out the playing space for them to do so, within the semi-circle of seated men. The stories acted by these men, all of them cab drivers, are simple. Joe goes home to his wife Edna and their two children. They have little money, and are short of food. Edna says that the union is doing nothing for them, and urges Joe to strike. 'Sweep out those racketeers like a pile of dirt.... Get brass toes on your shoes and know where to kick.' Miller, a laboratory assistant, is urged by his boss to work on poison gas, and also to spy on his laboratory chief. He refuses, is

sacked, becomes a cab driver. Young Sid and his girl Florence realize
that life holds nothing for them ('They want us trapped...the big
shot money men want us like that.'). A labour spy is brought on by
Fatt to convince us that the strike is wrong. He is exposed by people
in the audience. An efficient young doctor is sacked because he is a
Jew, decides to 'get some job to keep alive – maybe drive a cab'. The
leader of all these men is the little Italian cab driver, Lefty. Another
committee member is talking, when a man runs up the centre aisle
and says that they have found Lefty behind the car barns with a
bullet in his head. The Committee members shout to the audience,
'What's the answer?'

'Strike,' the audience replies.

'Louder,' the committee men say, and the audience shouts: 'Strike,
strike, strike!!!'

Waiting For Lefty was the first play put on at the newly-opened
Goldington Street theatre, preceded by the London Labour Choral
Union, a dance group performing 'A Comrade Has Died', and a
recitation from Paul Robeson. The performance roused the audience
to a high pitch of enthusiasm. 'Strike,' squeaked H.G. Wells, standing
and raising his fist, 'Strike, strike, strike.' The most successful Unity
plays employed a similar expressionist technique. In *Plant In The Sun*
(which came from America, like Odets's play) some East Side boys
working in a chocolate factory listen to Paul Robeson, a negro worker
who urges them to organize and join a union. Robeson is sacked, the
other workers plan a sit-down strike, one of the clerks informs on
them – and at the end of the play the men have downed tools and
are solid for the strike.

The activities of Unity were designed to induce militant action.
Even such experiments as the 'Living Newspaper' had this intention.
The Living Newspaper used a kind of documentary technique
developed in the United States, which was designed to interpret an
existing situation in fictional terms. So the first English Living Newspaper, 'Busmen', was linked with the bus strike taking place at the
time, and offered interpretations of the actual events, while using
extracts from speeches made by Ernest Bevin and others.

Behind all this, and behind the enthusiasm and originality that
made the failures of Unity more interesting than West End commercial successes, there was a mystique of Communism, found in such
things as the mass recitation of Ernst Toller's requiem for Karl
Liebknecht and Rosa Luxemburg, or the dramatized version of

Jack Lindsay's poem, 'Salute the Soviet Union', which ended

> Defend your homes,
> Defend the Soviet Union.
> Defend yourselves against the lords of war.
> Defend the citadel of peace and love.
> Defend the undaunted beacon of our hopes
> Here in the gathering fascist murk of hate.
> Salute the Soviet Union.

9

Surrealism and the AIA

Do not judge this movement kindly. It is not just another amusing stunt. It is defiant – the desperate act of men too profoundly convinced of the rottenness of our civilization to want to save a shred of its respectability....A nation which has produced two such superrealists as William Blake and Lewis Carroll is to the manner born. Because our art and literature is the most romantic in the world, it is likely to become the most superrealistic.

Herbert Read: *Catalogue of the International Surrealist Exhibition*

The International Surrealist Exhibition was held at the New Burlington Galleries from the 11th of June to the 4th of July, 1936. It was heralded by David Gascoyne's explanatory *A Short Survey of Surrealism* and André Breton's pamphlet, *What Is Surrealism?* Almost all of the important European Surrealists were represented, and a number of English artists whose work was influenced by Surrealism (in some cases very distantly) took part. On the opening day traffic in Bond Street and Piccadilly was held up by what one newspaper called 'the rush of young society' to the Exhibition. And it was not merely 'young society' that gathered to hear Herbert Read, standing uneasily on a springy sofa, tell them that those who loved art should thrill to the ushering in of a new epoch. 'Lovers of Lewis Carroll, Hieronymus Bosch and William Blake, and Suburbanites, filled the rooms,' the *Star* said. 'Lady Wimborne and Lady Juliet Duff were there. Osbert Sitwell, Sacha and Mrs Sacha Sitwell looked as if they understood everything. Baroness d'Erlanger and Constant Lambert were in the throng.' But the paper went on to say that most people regarded the Exhibition as a joke. 'Two characteristic comments were heard in the lift descending into Burlington Gardens. One was: "It's more laughable than Charley's Aunt"; the other was, "I'm going to have a brandy and soda and get a little fresh air in the National Gallery."'

Whether or not the Exhibition was a joke, it was certainly a practical success. More than 20,000 people went to look at the work of what was called in another paper the Marx Brothers of art. Certainly the Exhibition had some Marxian features. Salvador Dali (still surrealistically respectable, not yet transformed by anagram into Avida Dollars) wore a diving suit decorated like a Christmas tree, with a motorcar radiator cap on top of the helmet and plasticine hands stuck on the body of the suit to deliver, in French with a strong Spanish accent, a lecture which was relayed through loudspeakers. When the lecturer grew hot and asked that the helmet should be taken off, this was found to be difficult; it was finally prised up with the billiard cue he carried. Two Irish wolfhounds stood by docilely while Dali described his encounters with that phantom, Reality. A more tangible Surrealist Phantom wandered through the rooms in the form of a woman wearing a long white satin dress, with face and head obscured by a veil of roses. Long gloves covered her arms, and she carried in one hand a model leg filled with roses and in the other a raw pork chop. 'That get-up must be very hot,' one visitor said, and the Phantom, whose name was Sheila Legge, agreed. 'Yes, it is, very.' A bloater attached to a picture by Miro was removed by Paul Nash because of its unpleasant smell, and a fake picture signed D.S. Windle, a painting of a woman with a small imitation bird attached to the forehead by a piece of sponge and a fragment of cigarette by the mouth, was smuggled in by an academic portrait painter, and hung for a short time on the wall. Such diversions brought in the public. 'In terms of admission receipts, Surrealism has conquered London,' the *Daily Telegraph* said. A glass witch ball arrived at a later Exhibition. This had moustaches of various colours stuck around it. A paper frill on top enclosed a pig's trotter which held a cigarette. A newspaper cutting labelled it: 'Auden Receives Royal Medal.' This exhibit was not shown.

'Surrealism rests in the belief in the superior reality of certain forms of association neglected theretofore; in the omnipotence of the dream and in the disinterested play of thought. It tends definitely to do away with all other psychic mechanisms and to substitute itself for them in the solution of the principal problems of life.'

The omnipotence of the dream: how queer it seems, in the light of André Breton's words, that one of the principal arguments about Surrealism should have concerned its *political* implications. It was said that the Surrealists were 'literary' painters; that they bore some resemblances to the pre-Raphaelites; that their art was not automatic enough (a failing which has since been remedied by the *tachistes*), and so was 'impure': but, for most of the Surrealists, and for their English critics, the heart of the matter was the social meaning of the movement. To Breton the alignment of Surrealism and revolutionary Communism seemed obvious: 'Let it be clearly understood that for us, Surrealists, the interests of thought cannot cease to go hand in hand with the interests of the working class, and that all attacks on liberty, all fetters on the emancipation of the working class and all armed attacks on it cannot fail to be considered by us as attacks on thought likewise.' The twenty year old David Gascoyne expressed such revolutionary feelings in a poem called 'Baptism':

> Have had enough barbarity
> But enough too of illusion
> Dreams of peace.
>
> Walking in the water
> Or upon it
> With wet fingers on the brow
> And sombre eyes turned upwards
> No longer expectant but prepared
> Have had enough of war...
> Statement:
> *If you are with us you are red.*

And Charles Madge, the ideal intellectual revolutionary simpleton of the period, somehow managed to blend into a review of Gascoyne's book exultant praise of the Soviet Union:

'Everything is calmer now than it was immediately after the war or immediately before it, or even one hundred years before that. The "weight" and "tranquillity" of the USSR is being gradually imparted to the whole world. The British Fleet steams slowly and calmly through the blue Mediterranean. In the industrial areas a healing sunshine falls on acres of half-ruined factories. The more people try to create war, the more peaceful everybody becomes.'

To those involved in the politics of the Popular Front, however, such fanciful or metaphysical approaches seemed totally unacceptable. What place was there in the orderly equalitarian society of the future, a society in which the artist would work with the methodical precision of an engineer, for those who declared themselves in favour of the irrational, who praised Sade as surrealist in sadism and Baudelaire as surrealist in morals? The kind of 'freedom' aimed at by the Surrealists seemed to such people essentially reactionary: their art obscene or unintelligible, their politics dubious. 'They are the equivalent in art of the Fascist gangs in politics,' said J.B. Priestley. 'They stand for violence and neurotic unreason. They are truly decadent.' More calmly A.L. Lloyd analysed the movement in *Left Review*: 'If Surrealism were revolutionary it could be of use. But Surrealism is not revolutionary, because its lyricism is socially irresponsible.... Surrealism is a particularly subtle form of fake revolution.' The implication that art must necessarily be of direct social 'use' was made by Lloyd, and by other critics of the time, quite unquestioningly. It took an old-fashioned Socialist to be briskly dismissive. 'What the devil is Surrealism? Never heard of it,' said Bernard Shaw.

The impact of Surrealism on English painters and writers was slight. How much sympathy, after all, had Henry Moore, Julian Trevelyan, Paul Nash, for such a movement even though they showed work in the Exhibition? What did they do more than take fragments from it that seemed useful to them as deliberate and conscious artists? No English painter achieved the combination of meticulous detail with a deliberate disorder of the imagination that marked the most characteristic Surrealist work – that of de Chirico, Dali, Magritte, Tanguy; and most English Surrealist poems, like Hugh Sykes Davies's *Petron*, smell of library bindings. Even in the poems of David Gascoyne and Kenneth Allott, which approached most nearly the inconsequential gaiety or horror, the sensational but intuitively apt imagery, of good Surrealist verse, one can feel a directing mind. These writers are *using* Surrealism to obtain a freedom of word-association, and to create a confusion that still remains rational. Allott's charming 'Lullaby' is a good example of this sort of thing, a poem which without being Surrealist still could not have been written, or at least not written in this kind of way, without the movement's benevolent irrationality:

Say goodnight and step over the mountain
the cat will not stop washing his face
and the morning will be stepping up to you
to develop an intoxicating fluency
the voices of peasants, not singing to you.

Say goodnight and step out of the window
the night will spread its cold hands on your face
the world will still keep turning to the right
and in the darkness the turned-up whites of eyes
people dressing and undressing for some sake.

Say goodnight and close the door behind you
the wireless keeps on playing to the room
and if a gesture like the boyhood of Raleigh
and if a word who is there left to listen?
the timid footsteps dropping so far behind you.

Say goodnight, letting no further persuasion
flatter you from your sheets, letting the eye
turned inwards on yourself lose power to image
but hopeless now slip down into the sea
which has been waiting all along so patiently.

In the simplified, but still meaningful, line that I have been drawing, between aesthetic formalists on one side and social realists on
the other (although the formalists often showed traces of political
feeling and the social realists did not altogether ignore formalism in
their work) the Surrealists, in spite of Breton's fine words, must be
placed on the aesthetic side of the fence. 'Only disconnect,' they
seemed to be crying, 'Only disconnect, and the omnipotence of the
dream will take care of the political situation.' The social realists of
the time were to be found in the Artists International Association,
founded in 1933 in the recognition by some artists that, as its historian
Andrew Forge has said, 'the first need was for them to act as political
men'.

The three Jameses of *Left Review*, Boswell, Fitton and Holland,
provided part of the hard core of AIA, but the social realist movement
in the graphic arts was not identified with the Communist Party as
were Unity Theatre and *Left Review* in drama and literature, in spite
of exhortations by party-line critics like Anthony Blunt:

There are many kinds of painting which, at the level of painting
alone, seem to be revolutionary enough, but which have no roots
at all in the rising class. Abstract art and, above all, Surrealism,
belong to this type.... If we mean by revolutionary art the art

which most closely represents the ideas of the rising class, there can be no doubt that the true revolutionary art of today will be realistic.

Few artists were prepared to go all the way with such sentiments. The social realists of the AIA exhibited with Surrealists and abstractionists, and acknowledged that they too were taking politics seriously. The most enthusiastic AIA artists used their energies more directly in the service of the social struggle, that was all. They produced posters and banners for labour organizations, staged exhibitions of artists against Fascism, became political men. But around this core of committed artists there gathered many more who were in general sympathy with the social ideas of the AIA, but practised in their art a literal rather than a social realism. Such artists as Graham Bell, Victor Pasmore, William Coldstream and Robert Medley were committed in their art only to the realistic statement of appearances, without a hint of satire or of the idealized vision of the working class that was often satire's other face. The original social impulse behind the AIA was thus much softened, yet in this period when almost every interesting modern German artist was labelled by Hitler 'degenerate', these Euston Road artists also felt it necessary eventually to take a political stand. 'An artist who didn't take politics seriously then was a clown, a nobody': with this statement, made by one of their number, none of the artists connected with the AIA would have quarrelled.

10

The Left Book Club

One can see the period clearly by looking at three distinct movements, all of them mixing politics with literature, all involving various fractions of our pyramid: the revolution in technique which within a few years turned into a revolution in subject-matter, the attachment of artists to the Republican side in the Spanish Civil War, and the development of the Left Book Club. These things were inter-related: writers who had been looking for a cause in which to believe, a cause at once more specific and less dogmatic than a generalized belief in Communism, found it in the Spanish Civil War; artists who had been asking for a mass audience found one ready-made in the Left Book Club. But to accept these opportunities meant changes in the artists' attitudes. Many felt themselves bound to go out to Spain, or at least to produce or encourage Republican propaganda, while retaining an uneasy feeling that what they were doing hadn't much connection with their work as artists; and the ready-made Left Book Club audience had clear, and from the artists' point of view rather Philistine, ideas of what it wanted to read and look at. The positions of the artists who had in the very early Thirties declared themselves in sympathy with Communism became more and more uneasy as the decade went on. They found themselves compromising their art more and more in favour of 'society'.

The development of the Left Book Club was remarkable as a publishing feat, and as a social movement that could have occurred in no other place and time. It is always difficult to get people to subscribe in advance for books, even for popular fiction; that they should voluntarily subscribe in large numbers for Left wing books, most of them non-fiction, must have seemed to other publishers ludicrously unlikely when, in March 1936, Victor Gollancz announced his scheme. Yet before the publication of the first book, *France Today and the People's Front* by Maurice Thorez, the Club had more than 6,000 members; within six months there were well over 20,000; and a membership of 50,000 was reached within eighteen months.

The scheme had its origin in Gollancz's attempt, a few months earlier, to obtain a good subscription for a book which he regarded as important, R.D. Charques's *Profits and Politics*. His London traveller brought back ludicrously small orders, and when Gollancz asked him the reasons for the booksellers' refusal to subscribe, replied: 'They didn't say anything. They just laughed.' Perhaps Gollancz is exaggerating, but not very much, when he says that at this time ninety-nine booksellers out of 100 quietly boycotted books with Socialist tendencies. The booksellers' reaction was at once an insult to Gollancz's practical sense and an outrage to his idealism (two facets of his nature that blended very happily together during his remarkable publishing career). Certain that a large public existed for Left wing books, he prepared the scheme, and mentioned it to John Strachey as they came away together from the inaugural meeting of *Tribune*. Strachey was enthusiastic, and agreed to act as one of the selectors; Harold Laski was another; Gollancz himself the third.

The idea was broad and simple in outline. A member sent no money with his membership form; for half a crown a month he received, through his bookseller or direct, the choice of the month in a limp orange binding (the price to the public, in stiff covers, was seven shillings and sixpence or more), and he received also a copy of the *Left News*, which combined the characteristics of a Left wing magazine and a catalogue for advertising and discussing Gollancz books.

The purpose of the Left Book Club was, vaguely, to oppose Fascism: specifically to create a united front of Socialists, Communists and Liberals in this country. In France the Popular Front had achieved great successes at the polls, and had formed a Government; in England the Labour Party had gained nearly 100 seats in the 1935 election, but it still remained relatively powerless in Parliamentary terms, with a total representation of 154 against the National Government's 428. In his first editorial Gollancz drew the appropriate conclusions:

> France has, indeed, for a long time now been an example and an inspiration. It has not been merely a question of the drawing together of Socialists and Communists, or of the union of these two wings of the Labour movement with the Radicals: it has been rather a question of the mobilization of all men and women of good will against the threat of Fascism.

He went on to give details of the enthusiasm aroused by the idea of the club, particularly in working-class districts. 'In one place thirty unemployed are contributing a penny a month so that, jointly and through one of them, they may become a member: in another place we have been asked to give the names of twenty other members in the locality, so that a discussion group could be formed.'

The three selectors, Gollancz implied, were well-balanced. 'Professor Laski is a member of the Labour Party: Mr John Strachey is in broad sympathy with the aims of the Communist Party: and I am interested in the spreading of all such knowledge and all such ideas as may safeguard peace, combat Fascism, and bring nearer the establishment of real Socialism.'

Such were the intentions. In practice the Left Book Club's chief function was to serve as a propaganda machine for Communism.

An outrageous statement – I can hear Victor Gollancz indignantly saying it, pointing to the Socialists who found the club's discussion groups a tonic after the tedium of Labour Party meetings, the Liberals for whom the movement offered a hope for the future, the sense of unity that informed the whole. But let us consider the truth or falseness of the statement first, and then look at it in the context of the time.

During the Club's first year, four of the twelve books chosen actively promoted Communist policy: Thorez's book on the People's Front in France, Palme Dutt's *World Politics, 1918-1936*, Strachey's *The Theory and Practice of Socialism*, and *Spain in Revolt*, written by two members of the American Communist Party. It is likely that one or two of the other books chosen in this first year were written by Communists, but their propagandist purpose is not so evident. Two of the books chosen were in some degree unorthodox: Stephen Spender's *Forward From Liberalism* and George Orwell's *The Road to Wigan Pier*. Spender's book was unorthodox by the Club's standards because it was a long personal argument or self-examination, made by way of discussing the author's 'approach to Communism', rather than because of any overt criticism of Soviet Communist morality or tactics. Orwell's book was another matter, with its crude statements that the workers smelt, and that labour of the sort undertaken by miners was physically and spiritually degrading. Such statements were deeply shocking to those who adhered to the myth that some absolute virtue resided in the working class, and the anxious Selection Committee found it advisable to provide a preface, written by Gollancz.

It is in the long reviews and articles written for *Left News* that the Communist line of the Club shows through most clearly. Early issues contained a draft of the 1936 Soviet Constitution, a very full report of Thorez's speech to the French Communist Party congress, a long article by Strachey advocating a People's Front for Britain, and many reviews assessing current political books from a Communist point of view. They contained also articles by Ivor Montagu, 'The USSR Month by Month', which praised the Soviet Union's achievements, stressed the classless nature of its society, and explained such awkward matters as the Moscow Trials. The degree to which the Left Book Club was informed by Communist orthodoxy is best expressed by the fact that it would have been quite unthinkable that any work by Trotsky or his supporters should have been published by the Club, and very unlikely that any work seriously critical of the Soviet Union would have passed a selection committee which reached unanimous agreement about every book chosen. Gollancz, the most liberal of the selectors, would no doubt have rejected such books on the ground that they did nothing to 'safeguard peace, combat Fascism, and bring nearer the achievement of real Socialism'. Truth, once discovered, is always found to be monolithic, and Montagu explained Trotsky's role in an article on the Moscow trials of 1936: 'He is called counter-revolutionary, Fascist. This is right, though all his life he has been devoted, *in his belief*, to revolution and to socialism.'

Later it became necessary to correct this over-generous view, and to show that Trotsky had been a counter-revolutionary, an imperialist, a saboteur, a spy, for the whole of his adult life.

Truth is monolithic, truth is indivisible, truth may on any particular occasion be a necessary lie. These beliefs were widely held, although not expressed, in the Thirties, as they are at all times the beliefs of those engaged in propaganda for a cause. Thus, even if what Orwell said about the miners' lives and social attitudes was correct, many people on the Left would have felt that it should not be said at this particular time; even if Trotsky's criticisms of the Soviet Union were well-founded, they should not have been made. The threat of Fascism, the danger of war, were invoked as more important social realities than truths seen through the eyes of an individual; and the typical attitude of Left Book Club members could be expressed in a simple syllogism. A Popular Front is the only way of combating Fascism:

the support of the Soviet Union is necessary to such a Popular Front: therefore any criticism of the Soviet Union is in essence pro-Fascist. Even this syllogism does not go far enough, for the image of the Soviet Union was for many people during these years, Liberals and Socialists as well as Communists, a kind of positive hope. In a world where Fascism conquered or grew in every European country, where unemployment, misery and hunger were prevalent in Britain and the United States, the creation of the Soviet Union seemed the one certain progressive achievement in twenty years.

To understand is not to forgive: but we should not judge the Thirties from the different, easier standpoint of another age. The answer given at the time by a Socialist or Liberal who read the preceding paragraphs might well have been: *You say that the Left Book Club serves as a propaganda machine for Communism. What is so terrible about that?* Most of the Communists they knew were nice simple chaps, idealists; they bled as a Liberal bled, hungered as a Socialist hungered, wanted the same sort of new world as Socialists and Liberals, but had different ideas about the way to get it. The Communists were hard workers; good luck to them. An editorial in *Left News* discussed this question, and pointed out that Communists suggested subjects and were eager to write books, whereas Socialists and Liberals had to be badgered into doing so. The official Labour Party attitude to the club was one of stiff distrust. When it had been in existence for a little more than a year Hugh Dalton, on behalf of Transport House, refused the offer of two complete issues of *Left News* in which to expound official Socialist policy. The club, Dalton said, was 'consistently critical of the present leadership of the Party', and he suggested that the selection committee should include two or three representatives of the official viewpoint. This suggestion was declined. By a nice irony, the book chosen for that month was *The Labour Party in Perspective*, by C.R. Attlee.

It was inevitable that the focus of the Left Book Club upon the need for a Popular Front should antagonize official Labour opinion, but in any case the movement had a force and impetus that, in spite of its founders' denial of party political aims, made it in some ways a rival to the Labour Party. That suggestion for the foundation of a discussion group was like a signal. Six months later there were 150 discussion groups, within a year there were nearly 600, at the movement's peak there were well over 1,000, and loosely linked with them were Theatre, Film, Music and Poetry groups, all of them flourishing.

What did they talk about, the discussion groups? They varied a good deal: some, especially in the Home Counties, were largely social, coffee and biscuits in a member's house, people meeting to talk about new books and inveigh against the National Government and its foreign policy, enjoying the warm sense of shared feelings and common attitudes that keeps all minority movements together. Generally, though, there was a strong sense of purpose among those who came along to hear either a lecturer from headquarters or a local speaker talking about the choice of the month, or about a particular social problem. The discussion that followed was led by the few politically informed members of the audience, two or three Communists clashing with a Labour trade unionist about questions of ways and means, most of the others listening. The effect of such discussions upon an audience that shared the basic assumptions of speaker and debaters must have been very great – not necessarily by inducing any sort of immediate action, but by creating a climate of opinion in which automatic responses were engendered by certain words – capitalism, Fascism, landlords, unemployment. Not only responses, indeed: a whole mode of didactic arguments was half-consciously learned at these meetings, which could be seen in operation during the war at ABCA lectures, and which survived into the first years of Labour Government afterwards.

In *Coming Up For Air* George Orwell put down one of those caricatures of the audiences at a Left Book Club meeting that has, like other Orwellian caricatures, an uncomfortable truth about it:

> As well as I could from the back row I had a look at the audience. I suppose, if you come to think of it, we people who'll turn out on winter nights to sit in draughty halls listening to Left Book Club lectures (and I consider that I'm entitled to the 'we', seeing that I'd done it myself on this occasion) have a certain significance. We're the West Bletchley revolutionaries. . . . In the front row Miss Minns was sitting very upright, with her head cocked a little on one side, like a bird. The lecturer had taken a sheet of paper from under the tumbler and was reading out statistics about the German suicide-rate. You could see by the look of Miss Minns's long thin neck that she wasn't feeling happy. Was this improving her mind, or wasn't it? If only she could make out what it was all about! The other two were sitting there like lumps of pudding. Next to them a little woman with red hair was knitting a jumper. One plain, two purl, drop one and knit two together. The lecturer was describing

88 THE THIRTIES

how the Nazis chop people's heads off for treason and sometimes the executioner makes a boss shot. There was one other woman in the audience, a girl with dark hair, one of the teachers at the Council School. Unlike the others she was really listening, sitting forward with her big round eyes fixed on the lecturer and her mouth a little bit open, drinking it all in.

Just behind her two old blokes from the local Labour Party were sitting. One had grey hair cropped very short, the other had a bald head and a droopy moustache. Both wearing their overcoats. You know the type. Been in the Labour Party since the year dot. Lives given up to the movement. Twenty years of being blacklisted by employers, and another ten of badgering the Council to do something about the slums. Suddenly everything's changed, the old Labour Party stuff doesn't matter any longer. Find themselves pitchforked into foreign politics – Hitler, Stalin, bombs, machine-guns, rubber truncheons, Rome-Berlin axis, Popular Front, anti-Comintern pact. Can't make head or tail of it. Immediately in front of me the local Communist Party branch were sitting. All three of them very young....Next to these three another Communist was sitting. But this one, it seems, is a different kind of Communist and not quite-quite, because he's what they call a Trotskyist. The others have got a down on him. He's even younger, a very thin, very dark, nervous-looking boy. Clever face. Jew, of course. These four were taking the lecture quite differently from the others. You knew they'd be on their feet the moment question-time started. You could see them kind of twitching already. And the little Trotskyist working himself from side to side on his bum in his anxiety to get in ahead of the others.

These really were the sort of people who attended discussion group meetings – and the emphasis placed by Orwell upon the way in which the Communists, orthodox and dissident, leavened the whole mass, is exactly right. They were the people, also, who attended the great Left Book Club meetings held at the Albert Hall to appeal for a Popular Front, to protest against the Japanese invasion of China, to support the Spanish Republicans against Franco. Gollancz was in the chair: and on the platform were very often Strachey, Pollitt, Laski, Richard Acland, less often Stafford Cripps, Palme Dutt, Ellen Wilkinson and a few others. The *News Chronicle*'s A.J. Cummings attended the first of these meetings, in February 1937:

About 7,000 Left Book Club fans were there.... Though the 'platform' had a faint tinge of the Popular Front, I was left under no illusion about the inspiration of the Club and the kind of appeal it makes to seekers after knowledge. It is very Left indeed.

The name of Mr Harry Pollitt, the Communist leader, brought a bigger cheer than that of any other politician, and when he approached the microphone to say his piece the audience rose at him as if he were one of God's chosen.

The big meetings were not all held in London, nor were they all directly political. In Manchester the crowd filled the Free Trade Hall, and could have filled it again; and among the literary speakers at one meeting were Susan Ertz and Rose Macaulay, A.E. Coppard, Richard Church, L.A.G. Strong and Norman Collins. The movement grew and grew. In the *Left News* Gollancz said that the next target was 100,000 members.

11

Mass-Observation

You can have fun with this new science

Try a little Mass-Observation on your own account this week-end.

Daily Herald headlines

Mass-Observation was founded by Tom Harrisson, Humphrey Jennings and Charles Madge, a sociologist, a critic and a poet, in February 1937. The principal idea behind the movement was eventually to obtain, as Julian Huxley put it, 'some sort of scientific control of society, in place of the unscientific game of politics and the mere play of impersonal economic forces'. The knowledge that led to this scientific control was to be obtained through the activities of Mass-Observers, who were asked to write a report of what they saw and experienced in their ordinary lives on one day in every month. Within six months 1,300 observers were at work, producing reports like this:

> Coming home on a Midland Red 'Bus from Birmingham (a distance of approximately six miles) I was sitting on the front seat, near the large sliding door. There was a cold easterly wind blowing through the door, and after having some cigarette ash blown in my eyes, I touched the Conductor on the sleeve to attract his attention, and said 'May we have the door closed, Conductor?' He turned round and leant towards me in a confidential way, and then said in a most insolent manner 'Yes, when I'm ready to shut it!' I was too surprised to make any reply. The door remained open until I left the 'bus.

What possible interest could there be in such an encounter, possibly prejudiced, possibly even untrue? Charles Madge told us:

> The interest of the passage is (i) scientific, (ii) human, and therefore, by implication, (iii) poetic. It might equally well have

been told by the 'bus conductor or a third person. It is about human beings, but they are in a mechanical environment, which conditions their actions. Such observations as the insolent or 'confidential' manner of the 'bus conductor, though subjective, become objective because the subjectivity of the observer is one of the facts under observation.

This was what might be called the movement's theoretical side, for which Madge and Humphrey Jennings were chiefly responsible. The practical work done was of a very different kind. Hundreds of Mass-Observers made notes on Coronation Day, and the results of what they wrote were collected, and published in a fat book called *May the Twelfth*, a book almost unreadable in bulk but obviously of some documentary value. This was followed by research into social attitudes towards Armistice Day, a by-election, pubs, Air Raid Precautions. Mass-Observers descended in mass upon Bolton, wormed industriously through the town, and produced reports on it.

Julian Trevelyan has put down an entertaining account of his own activities upon this occasion: of how, under the furiously energetic direction of Tom Harrisson, Trevelyan was sent out to paint in the middle of the street (it was very important that he should paint in the *middle*), while William Empson made a report on the contents of a sweet shop window; of the facts amassed, 'reports on the orientation of the graves in St Mary's Cemetery, on the numbers, groupings, and sexes, of children in the Walkley Road Playground between 3.45 and 4.15 on June 15th, on conversations overheard at an all-in wrestling match, and so on'.

These were the two sides of Mass-Observation: the pretentious attempt to associate the movement with art and literature, and the realization that this was a technique of social research, which, whatever the early excesses caused by Harrisson's devotion to facts as things in themselves – facts like the conversations taking place in a town's public lavatories at 5.30 in the afternoon – had its use in social research. It was quickly realized also that the techniques could be useful in market research, in finding out something about the sort of food people liked to eat, the sort of soap they liked to use, the sort of clothes they liked to wear. In course of time, and it was not a very long time, Mass-Observation became much less an instrument for the scientific examination of human behaviour and much more a tool of consumer research. This, really, was what its founders had unsuspectingly hit upon, and if Mass-Observation helped to ensure the 'scientific control of society', it was in ways of which Julian Huxley had never dreamed. It was not the masses who had fun with a new science, but science that had its own sort of fun with the masses. That this implication of the movement should have been understood by so few people at the time seems now very strange. There is nothing more comic than the gullibility of the past.

In the movement's early days it was thought that Mass-Observation might in some way help in the scientific appreciation of literature, might even induce people to join the Popular Front. *Left Review* gave it a cautious blessing, and all sorts of artistic possibilities were canvassed. The wildest of these was the production of the Oxford Collective Poem, sponsored, as may be guessed, by the inimitable Madge.

The poem was written by twelve Oxford observers, all of them undergraduates, and it took a month to produce. They began by collecting images. At the end of every day one of them noted the scene, event, subject or phrase which had most occupied his mind, and after three weeks each of them had a list of some twenty images. These images overlapped and recurred in different persons, and sometimes there was a strong common feature in a series of different images. The observers tried to extract the essential details and form a single image. They were left with six such images:

The red garment of a woman
stone steps leading to a stone building
Shoes
Trees against the skyline
The ticking of a clock
Smoke issuing from a pipe

Next the twelve observers met, and composed a single pentameter line dealing with each of the chosen images. The lines were anonymous, and one line was selected by vote for each of the six images. Six lines emerged, and a week-end was allotted for incorporating these lines into a poem of not more than eighteen lines. The observers then submitted their still anonymous work for alteration by each of the eleven others, and at last another vote was taken on the basis of the final versions, to discover the best poem.

Believe the iron saints who stride the floods,
Lying in red and labouring for the dawn:
Steeples repeat their warnings; along the roads
Memorials stand, of children force has slain;
Expostulating with the winds they hear
Stone kings irresolute on a marble stair.

The tongues of torn boots flapping on the cobbles,
Their epitaphs clack to the crawling hour.
The clock grows old inside the hollow tower;
It ticks and stops, and waits for me to tick,
And on the edges of the town redoubles
Thunder, announcing war's climacteric.

The hill has its death like us; the ravens gather;
Trees with their corpses lean towards the sky.
Christ's corn is mildewed and the wine gives out.
Smoke rises from the pipes whose smokers die.
And on our heads the crimes of our buried fathers
Burst in a hurricane and the rebels shout.

It was noted with satisfaction that the poem was 'much more a
collective account of Oxford than of any single person in the group....
It has the sense of decay and imminent doom which characterizes
contemporary Oxford. This reflection of the immediate scene is what
is looked for in a collective poem.' And Madge remarked that the
collective poem 'differs from the individualist poem, which can only
be written once, under an exceptional stimulus (love, alcohol, political
passion, etc.), by an exceptional person. It requires no stimulus of
this kind. There is nothing to prevent this kind of collective poetry
from being turned out continuously – like daily journalism it is a
non-stop record of events.'

But the Oxford Collective Poem has had no successor.

12

Spain

I

THE DECEIVED

The background to the Spanish Civil War of 1936 to 1939 is examined in detail by Hugh Thomas in his excellent history of the war. One or two dates and figures may be helpful here. At the elections in February 1936, the Popular Front gained a clear majority in terms of seats over its combined opponents. The Front was composed of several Left wing parties, including a small number of Communists – they won seventeen seats in the election, out of a total of two hundred and seventy-eight seats gained by the Left. Manuel Azana of the Republican Left party became Prime Minister. Socialists and radicals of all kinds were released from prison.

Azana's Government was a moderate one in terms of Spanish politics, but on the Left and Right equally he was seen as another Kerensky, who would be swept aside as the revolutionary tide rose. Plans for a revolt headed by Right wing Generals were in preparation almost before the election was over, and Left wing plans to replace Azana were not lacking. Within a few months he had become the influential but less powerful President of the Republic, and Largo Caballero was the Prime Minister. Caballero was nominally a Socialist, but he made speeches calling for the dictatorship of the proletariat, and he refused to take office unless the Communists entered the Government.

The Generals' revolt in mid-July 1936, and the Government resistance to it, made Spain a battleground of hope and conscience for Left wing groups in every country, and the country soon became a literal battleground for some of them as well. The first move to organize a British group of volunteers was made by two east London garment workers named Sam Masters and Nat Cohen, both of them members of the Communist Party. Masters and Cohen were cycling in France. They crossed the frontier to Barcelona and formed the Tom Mann Centuria. Felicia Browne, an artist, was the first person from this country to be killed. She had gone to Barcelona to attend a sports festival, enrolled in the militia, and was shot through the head on the Aragon front in late August. She also was a member of the Communist Party.

The struggle in Spain was the peak of the Popular Front movement, and to many of those involved in it, particularly among the Artists and Pragmatists of our pyramid, it was the turning point of their lives. To those uncertain of their course, doubtful about the Moscow Trials but feeling still that emotional adherence to the Soviet Union which so many 'progressives' of the time wore like a trade union badge, and feeling above all a need to identify themselves with some cause unquestionably good, it seemed that the future of Europe was being drawn on the map of Spain. 'The issues are very simple,' a young poet said to me at a party. 'This is a struggle between the forces of good in the world and the forces of evil,' and many people in Britain were grateful to recognize in the Spanish struggle something very much like that. Legality was on the side of the Republicans, and this was a point of great importance to their sympathisers among the Audience. This was a Government properly elected, and not a Communist Government but one representing a dozen different shades of political opinion. Opposed to this democratically elected Government were rebel generals, Fascists, Moorish mercenaries. The rebels were being armed with German and Italian guns and rifles, so that the British Government's declaration in favour of a policy of non-intervention was in effect support of the rebellion. J.B. Priestley expressed accurately the feelings of many liberal sympathisers.

There was a time when the whole of the Press would not have hesitated to denounce any military clique that tried to wrest power from an elected Government. But now it seems that the Fascism that is turning Europe into an armed camp has found a voice – or, rather, several very powerful voices – in Britain. It is the duty of all of us who believe in the right of people to govern themselves to answer these voices, to proclaim the truth against a thousand lies.

The policy of non-intervention, Stephen Spender said, was 'more grotesquely, obviously and dangerously a support of interference by the Fascist powers than was the arms embargo in the Abyssinian conflict a present of munitions and victory to Italy'. Committees were formed, as it seemed almost overnight, to provide arms and medical aid for Republican Spain, to investigate allegations of Fascist atrocities, to discover the nature and extent of foreign intervention. Franco was receiving help from Portugal, and Louis Golding urged Republican sympathizers to drink no port. Francis Meynell, founder of the Nonesuch Press, in a speech typical of many made at the time, told his audience to 'Give, give until it hurts, to the Spanish Medical Aid Fund. We are five hundred miles from Spain, but only three miles from Aldgate' (and Fascist demonstrations). 'Give – give until it hurts. It will not hurt so much as a bullet in the belly.' The AIA started a scheme called Portraits for Spain; the fee paid for such portraits, or part of it, went to Spanish Relief funds.

But for many, to give until it hurt was not enough. From early September onwards a steady stream of British volunteers flowed out to Spain, at first without difficulty and later, when the British Government imposed an embargo on volunteers, by various stratagems. There are no reliable statistics available about the number of British volunteers, their ages, or their class and political affiliations, but it is likely that at least half of them were Communists. Most of the volunteers joined the British battalion of the Communist-controlled International Brigade, a smaller number enlisted with the Anarchists or the near-Trotskyist POUM. Their casualties were extremely heavy. Of the 2,000 volunteers for the International Brigade nearly 500 were killed, and another 500 were seriously wounded. The total number of British volunteers who reached Spain certainly did not exceed 4,000 and there can be no doubt that most of them were militant members of the working class. 'For the most part they were workers, though some were intellectuals from the middle classes,' says the Communist William Rust of those who joined the International Brigade. 'In politics, many were Left wing Labour and Communist, but other tendencies were moderate and liberal, while the views of some could hardly be defined at all.' Tom Wintringham, who was a Captain in the International Brigade, said that his companions were very much like the men you meet at any football match, and still more like the men who march in a May Day procession. Most were English, many Scotch, some Irish, a few Welsh. Some three per cent were Jews. A few were adventurers, and between a quarter and an eighth of them were unemployed.

What were they looking for, those members of the intelligentsia who went out and fought beside these men? One unconscious motive behind their action was the wish to obtain that contact with the working class which was denied to them in their ordinary lives. The practical difficulties of association with what was, in the Thirties mythology, a great source of good, were great. What meeting point was there between poets like John Cornford and Julian Bell, scientists like Lorimer Birch, writers like Hugh Slater, and miners from Durham, cotton-workers from Lancashire? War melts away the barriers between classes, and also creates shared interests, bonds of knowledge and affection. Spain gave, then, a comradeship of class with class; but it gave more than this. For a few months at the start of the Civil War, Spain seemed the image of a new world. For those who lived in Britain, what did 'political activity' mean? Picketing a Fascist meeting, selling papers in the street, arguing at the local Left Book Club discussion group. To be transferred suddenly from this atmosphere to a country where political movements were taken with the deepest seriousness, where individual actions and beliefs no longer appeared trivialities beside the vast monolith of capitalist society, seemed like the realization of a dream. There is something dreamlike about the first sight of Spain as it is recorded by John Sommerfield, one of the earliest volunteers:

The sky began faintly to undarken and we could see that we were in a harbour with a long stone quay; all around were the grey shapes of battleships. Most were British and seeing them we were filled with a sense of shame and indignation. It was illogical, perhaps, but the arrogance of their grey, deadly efficiency, the menace of their guns, seemed yet another threat to the harassed Spanish people.... Then the anchor was got up, we moved slowly forward towards the quay and everyone went to fetch their packs. Now we could see the bright stucco houses and the palms, the shuttered cafés, the little yellow trams, the long white road winding up the mountain to the fortress. On the way were men in overalls carrying rifles, some dock labourers, a youth with an Anarchist cap and a Sam Browne belt with an enormous revolver stuck in it. The water gap between the side of the ship and the quay swirled and narrowed and we looked right down into the eyes of the men standing there. Over the customs house three flags floated, the Republican and the Anarchist colours and a yellow hammer and sickle on blazing red. This was Spain.

And to many volunteers it seemed, again in these early months, that in Spain the classless society of which they had talked so much, and which they reluctantly knew not to exist as yet in the Soviet Union, had been created here in one decisive stroke. In December George Orwell arrived in Barcelona.

When one came straight from England the aspect of Barcelona was something startling and overwhelming. It was the first time that I had ever been in a town where the working class was in the saddle. Practically every building of any size had been seized by the workers and was draped with red flags or with the red and black flag of the Anarchists; every wall was scrawled with the hammer and sickle and with the initials of the revolutionary parties; almost every church had been gutted and its images burnt. Churches here and there were being systematically demolished by gangs of workmen. Every shop and café had an inscription saying that it had been collectivized; even the boot-blacks had been collectivized and their boxes painted red and black. Waiters and shopwalkers looked you in the face and treated you as an equal. Servile and even ceremonial forms of speech had temporarily disappeared.... And it was the aspect of the crowds that was the queerest thing of all. In outward appearance it was a town in which the wealthy classes had practically ceased to exist. Except for a small number of women and foreigners there were no 'well-dressed' people at all. Practically everyone wore rough working-class clothes, or blue overalls or some variant of the militia uniform. All this was queer and moving. There was much in it that I did not understand, in some ways I did not even like it, but I recognized it immediately as a state of affairs worth fighting for.

Those who died in this sunlight of belief were in a sense the lucky ones. Among them were Christopher Caudwell and Ralph Fox, the chief British Communist aesthetic theoreticians ('His broad humanism and commonsense were a valuable corrective against ultra-Left enthusiasm,' said a pompous note on Fox in *Left Review*); the greatly talented John Cornford, who fought at first with the POUM and then with the International Brigade, and two other young poets, Julian Bell and Charles Donnelly; David Guest, Lorimer Birch, and Lewis Clive, who had rowed for Oxford in the boat race, and won the double sculls for England in the Olympic Games. Some, like

Esmond and Giles Romilly, were forced to return to England against their will, with their illusions still strong upon them. Many of the officers – Wintringham, the Brigade's Chief of Staff Malcolm Dunbar, and Hugh Slater, who was the first political commissar, later commander of the anti-tank battery and later still Brigade Chief of Operations – survived.

The war had no clarifying effect upon the feelings and actions of the Auden Group. Auden went to Spain, certainly, as a stretcher bearer in an ambulance unit, but he returned home after only two months, and, according to Spender, never spoke of his visit. The distaste shown in his work for people 'like the men you meet at any football match' has already been noticed. It is possible, and even likely, that in Spain Auden was confronted unavoidably with this feeling of distaste for all those with whom he was unable to make contact by taste or training, and that these weeks in Spain were in some way a decisive experience for him. It is true that after his return he wrote 'Spain', upon the whole the best poem in English concerned with the Civil War: but it is a poem, one is bound to say, which might have been written by a man who had never set foot in Spain, a triumph of Auden's poetic genius from which all that he felt in the country seems to have been excluded:

On that arid square, that fragment nipped off from hot
Africa, soldered so crudely on inventive Europe;
    On that tableland scored by rivers,
Our thoughts have bodies; the menacing shapes of our fever

Are precise and alive. For the fears which made us respond
To the medicine ad. and the brochure of winter cruises
    Have become invading battalions;
And our faces, the institute-face, the chain-store, the ruin

Are projecting their greed as the firing squad and the bomb.
Madrid is the heart. Our moments of tenderness blossom
    As the ambulance and the sandbag;
Our hours of friendship into a people's army.

The translation of events in Spain into the terms of individual psychology seems here disagreeably superficial, and 'Spain' lacks altogether the immediacy and actuality of the poems about Spain written by Spender, Cornford and others. 'Spain' saw, very nearly, the end of Auden as a poet who wished to align his art with a social movement. Ahead of him lay the grandeurs and follies of an eccentric individualism, and a determination to re-write his own poetic past, so that, in 'Spain', there is no longer any reference to a people's army and 'the conscious acceptance of guilt in the necessary murder' has become 'the conscious acceptance of guilt in the fact of murder'. The process has been a painful one to watch.

It is in the activities of Stephen Spender, activities later described by him with the most disarming self-critical humour and candour, that the agonies, the confusions and hesitations felt by the Auden Group in relation to Spain, are most clearly shown. When the war began, Spender paid a visit to the Communist Party's general secretary, Harry Pollitt, at Pollitt's invitation. Whatever their disagreements about the Moscow Trials, Pollitt said, didn't they agree about Spain? Wouldn't Spender support the Communists in their effort to help the Spanish Republic? Wouldn't he join the Party? Spender felt that he could not refuse, particularly when Pollitt offered space for an article in the *Daily Worker* in which he could put his point of view. The article appeared, Spender became a Party member. He was disconcerted to find that membership solved no political or emotional problems, more disconcerted still to find that Communism had 'taken' violently in the case of an even more recent convert, his friend Jimmy Younger, and that Younger was going to fight with the International Brigade. Spender was unwilling to join the Brigade, but when he received a letter offering him a post as head of English broadcasting at the radio station of the Socialist Party in Valencia, he accepted it at once. When he got to Valencia he found that the Socialist station had been abolished, and he devoted much time and energy to an attempt to get Jimmy Younger out of the International Brigade. Jimmy had decided that he did not want to die for Spain, that he did not want to die at all, that he was really a Pacifist, an ordinary chap who hated war. Spender paid a visit to the front line ('We make a point of not allowing our front-line visitors to be killed,' said the Brigade Chief of Operations, Major Nathan, who was killed himself within a few months), and thereafter was used, like many other writers, as a propagandist for the Republican cause.

So enthusiasm turned to something very much like farce. In Spender's autobiography there is a memorably witty and cynical account of the Writers' Congress held in Madrid in the summer of 1937. The

delegates went there to show support for the Spanish Republic but
one concealed purpose of the Congress was to denounce André Gide,
who had just published *Retour de l'U.R.S.S.*, in which he sharply
criticized the Soviet Union. The Russian delegates therefore confined
themselves to praising the Soviet Union's support of the Republic,
and to attacks on Trotsky and Gide. This was the real business of
the Congress, and providing it was carried out the delegates might
be allowed their bread and circuses. They rode about in Rolls-Royces,
ate well, made speeches, drank champagne, and in several cases
became infected with a hysterical sense of self-importance. Spender
tells stories of André Chanson, secretary of the French delegation,
who said that he must leave shelled Madrid at once, because if he
should be killed France was bound to declare war on Franco, and
that would lead to world war; of an English Communist novelist who
claimed, with satisfaction (although probably untruthfully), that he
had arranged for a cowardly member of the Brigade to be sent to a
place where he was certain to be killed; of the graciously forbidding
Communist lady novelist who began her remarks to Spender with
'Wouldn't it be less selfish, comrade,' and then went on to outline
some course of action convenient to herself. Spender sees his own
conduct with a similarly disillusioned eye:

> I was secretly offended when I was not called upon to speak
> (though presumably I had nothing to say since I remember
> scarcely a word of any public utterances by myself or any other
> member of the Congress). Sometimes, when I was sitting in a
> conference hall, I saw a camera pointed in my direction, or an
> artist, with pencil poised above drawing block, looking towards
> me. Then, hating myself, I kept very still, until I noticed that the
> photographer was really concerned with Malraux or Neruda or
> Alberti who happened to be sitting nearby.

It is curious, after reading this passage in Spender's autobiography,
to go back to his notes made on the Congress at the time, and published in *New Writing*. They express nothing of his later feeling that
the Congress 'had something about it of a Spoiled Children's Party';
his account of the congress, and of the delegates' other activities in
Spain, has a romantic and heroic flavour. There is nothing here about
the selfishness of the lady novelist, nothing about the Communist
writer who boasted that he had sent somebody to his death, nothing

about Chanson's insistence on leaving Madrid because his death might precipitate a world war (a similar story is told, but with quite a different emphasis and effect). Above all, there is nothing about the fact that the 'hidden theme' of the Congress, as Spender later calls it, was 'the Stalinists versus André Gide'. The only mention of Gide is in connection with a conversation Spender had with the Catholic poet José Bergamin. Spender felt that Bergamin was the only person at the Congress who had a right to criticize Gide, because Bergamin had 'a mind of even greater honesty, a mind which sees not merely the truth of isolated facts which Gide observed in the USSR, but the far more important truth of the *effect* which Gide's book is going to have.'

If I were asked whether it is not purely Stephen Spender's own affair that he has changed his mind about the Congress – or told, a little more subtly, that the Spender of 1951 was a different person from the Spender of 1937 and so wrote of the Congress differently – what should I say? Why, simply that the earlier version was evidently in some ways an outrage to Spender's own nature, that, like so many people at the time, he reported what he wished to believe. Is it not unconsciously a most revealing phrase, that one which compares the truth of what Gide saw with the 'truth' of the effect of his book? And has there been another time in the past hundred years when a writer of Spender's quality could have brought himself to believe that the truth one saw with one's own eyes should be suppressed? Artists like Spender were forced into the position of maintaining that the cause itself was so virtuous that a certain degree of untruthfulness in supporting it was perfectly pardonable.

The most satisfying experiences in Spain undoubtedly belonged to those who went out to fight. The others who stayed on the fringe, made speeches and attended Congresses, felt, in the reluctance to fight, something vitally true to their own characters, yet were at the same time ashamed; shocked by the evidence of Communist ruthlessness around them, they were also moved by the wish to submit themselves to this dread authority. This unsatisfied desire to merge their own identities in some greater reality marks the attitudes of Artists and Pragmatists throughout the period, and for many of them the activities they undertook on behalf of the Spanish Republic intensified rather than assuaged their self-dissatisfaction.

II

THE DECEIVERS

When Arthur Koestler visited Paris a fortnight after the war began, he naturally went to see his friend Willy Muenzenberg, who was at this time the head of 'the Comintern's West-European AGITPROP Department'. Muenzenberg's propagandist activities were manifold. He had just formed the Committee for War Relief for Republican Spain and the Spanish Milk Fund, and was in process of forming the Committee of Inquiry into Foreign Intervention in the Spanish War. These, and several other Committees, were Communist-front organizations: that is, most of the people who served on them did so in good faith (Philip Noel-Baker, Lord Faringdon, Eleanor Rathbone and other non-Communists were members of the Commission of Inquiry into Alleged Breaches of the Non-Intervention Agreement in Spain), but the organizers were realistic Communists, who knew exactly what they wanted done, and how to do it. Koestler was told that he should make a trip to Franco's headquarters as a newspaper correspondent. He already held a card for the ultra-Conservative Hungarian paper, *Pester Lloyd*, and now Otto Katz, Muenzenberg's second-in-command, made a telephone call to London and arranged within an hour that Koestler should be a *News Chronicle* correspondent also. Would the *Chronicle* pay for the journey? Koestler asked, and learned that the 'Committee' would pay.

So began Koestler's work as a Communist undercover man in Spain, work which is especially interesting because it shows a section of the great Communist honeycomb in the country, with all its members working busily, although sometimes at cross-purposes with each other. Here is Koestler writing *Spanish Testament*, which is to be published as a Left Book Club choice, here is Otto Katz working in the same flat, also on a propaganda book about Spain, here is Muenzenberg criticising them.

> He would pick up a few sheets of the typescript, scan through them, and shout at me: 'Too weak. Too objective. Hit them! Hit them hard! Tell the world how they run over their prisoners with tanks, how they pour petrol over them and burn them alive. Make the world gasp with horror. Hammer it into their heads. Make them *wake up*.'

Koestler did his best to make them wake up. He was arrested when
Franco captured Malaga, and was sentenced to death. He was saved
by an immense propaganda campaign, which had some Communist
inspiration but gathered a momentum that had nothing to do with
the Communists, based on Koestler's position as the presumedly
Liberal correspondent of a Liberal newspaper. (Two other *News
Chronicle* correspondents in Spain, William Forrest and John
Langdon-Davies, were also Communists at this time.) Fifty-eight
Members of Parliament, nearly half of them Conservatives, protested
to Franco; authors' and journalists' associations protested also, and
so did many political, cultural and religious bodies. The British
Government itself addressed representations to Franco on behalf of
the Liberal newspaper man. Otto Katz produced some fictitious
stories about Koestler's ill-treatment in prison. When at last he was
exchanged for the wife of one of Franco's fighter pilots, it was of
course necessary for Koestler to go on playing his part. 'By the logic
of circumstances the fiction of the *bona fide* Liberal journalist had to
be maintained,' and it was maintained in the *News Chronicle* and
elsewhere, in spite of the actor's increasing distaste for the part he
was playing. He made a four weeks' lecture tour for the Left Book
Club, to talk about the political and military situation in Spain. Koestler was in a state of suppressed dissatisfaction with Communism,
but his heretical answers to questions about the character and fate
of the POUM, which had been suppressed by the Communists in
Spain, were regarded merely as proof of an over-tender conscience.
'The exploitation of the war by Moscow for its own purposes, the
activities of the GPU and SIM behind the front-lines, did not enter
the picture. Any mention of these subjects would have met with
incredulity and indignation.' The Duchess of Atholl, the Conservative
who wrote an introduction to *Spanish Testament*, was, Koestler says,
the only person who at this time asked him whether he was a member
of the Communist Party. 'Your word is enough for me,' she said,
when he denied it.

In his autobiography Koestler says nothing about the reports he
sent back to the *News Chronicle*, but it is obvious that these reports
contained just as much truth as the requirements of the Party
demanded, and that all the newspaper men or 'liberals' or 'impartial
observers' who were at this time members of the Communist Party
practised a tremendous deception on the British public. Chief among
them was the irrepressible Claud Cockburn, who (as 'Frank Pitcairn')

wrote for the *Daily Worker*, and in his own identity edited the Communist news sheet called *The Week*, which professed to give information about political developments in Europe and America, much of which came straight from Cockburn's fertile brain. As Pitcairn he wrote a book called *Reporter in Spain*, which was accepted by many others besides Communists as a moving and convincing account of conditions in Spain. In *Homage to Catalonia* George Orwell detailed the inaccuracies of which Frank Pitcairn was guilty in dealing with the suppression of the POUM in Barcelona, the wholly fictitious account of tanks, scores of machine guns and thousands of rifles used by the POUM in what Pitcairn called a Trotskyist attempt to seize power. Orwell felt nominally compelled to assume Pitcairn's good faith, and to say simply that he was strangely mistaken, but there is no need to make any such assumption today, after the publication of Cockburn-Pitcairn's volumes of autobiography.

In one of them he tells how he arrived in Paris from Spain, and telephoned Otto Katz at the office of the Spanish Republican Press Agency, Agence Espagne. 'What I want now,' Katz said, 'is a tip-top, smashing, eye-witness account of the great anti-Franco revolt which occurred yesterday at Tetuan, the news of it having hitherto been suppressed by censorship.' Cockburn-Pitcairn said he had never been in Tetuan, and had not heard of the revolt. 'Not the point at all,' Katz said. 'Nor have I heard of any such thing.' He explained that a crucial moment had been reached in the supply of arms to the Republicans. A consignment of arms was waiting on the French frontier, and if a suitable jolt was administered to the French Government, in the form of a hint that Franco's defeat might be imminent, the arms would be let through. What better place for a revolt than Tetuan in Spanish Morocco, which had been the starting place of Franco's rebellion? They set to work.

Our chief anxiety was that, with nothing to go on but the plans in the guidebooks, which were without contours, we might have democrats and fascists firing at one another from either end of an avenue which some travelled night-editor might know had a hump in the middle. The fighting, accordingly, took place in very short streets and open squares.... Katz was insistent that we use a lot of names, of both heroes and villains, but express uncertainty over some of them – thus in the confusion of the struggle outside the barracks it had been impossible to ascertain whether the Captain

Murillo who died so gallantly was the same Captain Murillo who,
a few months ago in Madrid....In the end it emerged as one of
the most factual, inspiring, and at the same time sober pieces of
war reporting I ever saw.

Léon Blum read it and talked excitedly of its significance. The arms
got through.

Reading such accounts, noticing the pleased casualness with which
Cockburn-Pitcairn now puts them down, reading Koestler's stories
of the Potemkinised villages through which celebrities were taken to
convince them that the Republicans did not destroy churches (and
comparing what Cockburn-Pitcairn and Koestler and Spender say
now with their pious sentiments at the time), considering the solemn
farce of the fact that the International Brigade had its Major Attlee
Company to express solidarity with the forces that its Communist
leaders were doing their best to destroy, one is tempted to suggest,
with a cynicism equal to Cockburn-Pitcairn's own, that perhaps the
whole Spanish conflict was unreal, that Spain was nothing more than
a trial run for war, a ground on which the Fascist forces of Germany
and Italy could meet the forces sent and used by the Soviet Union,
and could test the efficacy of air bombardment, the uses of tanks and
anti-tank weapons: that this was nothing more than a great military
exercise in which the targets ran blood instead of sawdust. How much
would 'the conscience of the civilized world', as it was often called
at that time, accept? Would it accept an air attack on Madrid, a city
with no air defences, the ruined city and the 1000 killed? Would it
accept the wanton destruction of Guernica, without anything more
than verbal protest? It would? Then a principle had been established,
and Lidice could be destroyed, London, Coventry, Berlin, Dresden,
and a hundred other cities bombed, and still it could be claimed with
a straight face that these activities were undertaken in the defence of
civilized values.

That is what one is tempted to suggest, as the layers of deceit are
painfully peeled away, but it is not the truth, or it is not the most
important truth. The deepest tragedy for the intelligentsia involved
in the Spanish struggle was that truths and lies were inextricably
tangled, that the deceivers were also the deceived.

'When the International Brigades saved Madrid on November 8,

1936, we all felt that they would go down in history as the defenders of Thermopylae did; and when the first Russian fighters appeared in the skies of battered Madrid, all of us who had lived through the agony of the defenceless town felt that they were the saviours of civilization.' This was written by an Arthur Koestler who had been engaged for years in Communist undercover work, and who was carrying out deliberate deceptions in Spain: yet there is no doubt that Koestler believed what he said. As the struggle in Spain continued for month after month, as year succeeded year, the foreigners involved in it developed inevitably their own kind of doublethink, by which they justified actions seen by themselves and witnessed by others which would have horrified them at the time they first came out to Spain.

Now the same night falls over Germany
And the impartial beauty of the stars
Light from the unfeeling sky
Oranienburg and freedom's crooked scars.
We can do nothing to ease that pain
But prove the agony was not in vain.

England is silent under the same moon,
From Clydeside to the gutted hills of Wales.
The innocent mask conceals that soon
Here too our freedom's swaying in the scales.
Oh, understand before too late
Freedom was never held without a fight.

Freedom is an easily spoken word
But facts are stubborn things. Here, too, in Spain
Our fight's not won till the workers of all the world
Stand by our guard on Huesca's plain,
Swear that our dead fought not in vain,
Raise the red flag triumphantly
For Communism and for liberty.

John Cornford, who wrote these lines, was killed on his twenty-first birthday, before the war was six months old, and there is about the few poems that he wrote in Spain the sort of eager innocence that was noticed by Koestler among the Left Book Club audiences. There is the same sort of feeling in Tom Wintringham's poem, 'Granien':

Too many people are in love with death
And he walks thigh-proud, never sleeps alone;
Consider him neighbour and enemy, both
Hated and usual, best avoided when
Best known.

Weep, weep, weep! say machine-gun bullets, stating
Mosquito-like a sharper note near by;
Hold steady the torch, the black, the torn flesh, lighting,
And the searching probe; carry the stretcher; wait,
Eyes dry.

Our enemies can praise death and adore death;
For us endurance, the sun; and now in this night
The electric torch, feeble, waning, but close-set,
Follows the surgeon's fingers; we are allied with
This light.

Wintringham left Spain in November 1937, badly wounded and
three and a half stone lighter than when he first crossed the Pyrenees.
Such poems as these prompted a wit to answer the question asked
in the early nineteen forties: 'Where are the war poets?' with the
reply: 'Killed in Spain.' But the fine simplicity of feeling that marks
the poems written in the early months of the war could not survive
the things the intelligentsia saw in Spain as the war went on, and the
Communist Party tightened its grip on the country, carrying out
unofficial purges like that in which the POUM leaders were fetched
out of prison by an unidentified group of men, taken towards Madrid
and shot. Desperately they tried to justify this Communist control
by saying that the Communists were the best organized force in Spain,
and that to win the war it was necessary to have a unified command:
but by their public acquiescence in what they secretly disapproved
the deceived became the deceivers, so that in the end those who had
fought, and even those who had participated in the war as slightly
as Auden, Spender and Isherwood, found that in some sense they
had been corrupted by the part they had played. Some essential truth
about Spain, and about life itself, remained untold in their work, and
they had been manœuvred into a position where they were unable
to tell it, just as Koestler, freed from prison and lionized by English
liberals, found himself committed to telling lies.

I have said already that those who fought and died in Spain, with the bloom of their illusions untouched, were the lucky ones. Of the others, some hardened into Party functionaries; some, like Muenzenberg and Katz, were purged; some, like Slater and Wintringham, found themselves distrusted everywhere when they had left the Party. For those less directly involved, Spain, which had seemed at first a symbol of faith and goodness, an arena 'where a cause representing a greater degree of freedom and justice than a reactionary opposing one, gained victories', as Spender put it, turned slowly into one more defeat in the long line that had begun in 1933 with Hitler's triumph. It became also a test which, as individuals, they had somehow failed: a defeat, in its way final as are all defeats. After Spain, and indeed before the end came in Spain, there was little left of the Thirties movement but a feeling of resignation and a sense of guilt.

13

Heresy, Guilt, Munich

The art, the ideas, the politics of a decade are never so nicely self-contained as historians like to make them. The Nineties contained Kipling as well as the artists who contributed to *The Savoy*; and, more than this, the Kiplingesque attitude and that of the Savoyards both sprang from the same social situation. So the heretics of the Thirties, Wyndham Lewis, George Orwell, Robert Graves, all represented something important in the decade. They showed the other side of the Popular Front medal, whereas the social ideas and literary activities of T.S. Eliot (say) became steadily more remote from what was going on.

> We are swept away by a strange tide.
> Did Mr Eliot at Hyde
> Park Corner in 1917 boarding a bus
> Foresee it? He was not born in us
>
> But we in him.
> He gave us a voice, straightened each limb,
> Set us a few mental exercises
> And left us to our own devices.
>   Gavin Ewart

Those devices were emphatically not Mr Eliot's. He bequeathed a style rather than an attitude, and the Christianity of the *Four Quartets* appeared not so much uncongenial as meaningless to the Thirties writers. Eliot's technical mastery as poet and dramatist was acknowledged, but in the realm of ideas he was regarded as an eccentric reactionary unlikely to do much harm. The writings of Wyndham Lewis and Orwell, however, aroused the fiercest social opposition. They became, as the decade went on, more and more like some terrible *memento mori*. 'If we were not as we are, if we had not been saved, this,' orthodox Artists and Pragmatists thought with a shiver as they contemplated the Fascist monster Lewis and the Trotskyist demon Orwell, 'is what we might have become.' Both Lewis and Orwell suffered from delusions of persecution, yet it is true also that they both were writers actually persecuted for their expression of heterodox and inconvenient opinions. The suggestion that Lewis's works should be boycotted through Left Book Club groups was seriously canvassed at one time, and Orwell believed that after the publication of *Homage to Catalonia* his work was rejected in many places where earlier it would have been received. Lewis was not a Fascist, although he wrote one article for the *British Union Quarterly*, and H.G. Wells's description of Orwell as 'a Trotskyist with flat feet' was more witty than truthful. They were pilloried because they presented such uncomfortable interpretations of the same image of reality that acted as model for the Popular Front orthodoxy.

'Politically, I take my stand exactly midway between the Bolshevist and the Fascist,' Lewis wrote at the time when he was most obviously sympathetic to Fascism. 'The gentleman on my left I shake with my left hand, the gentleman on my right with my right hand. If there were only one (as I wish there were) I'd shake him with *both* hands.' This equating of Left and Right, this implication that violent change was the important thing and that the political form of the ensuing dictatorship did not greatly matter, horrified the Audience. Was it for this that they had reluctantly supported the 'good' use of force that was to defeat the 'bad' use of force by reactionaries? To be told that the force itself, the violence, was what mattered, and that once the slate had been wiped clean the benevolent dictator, Adolf, Benito or Josef, would be able to make a world fit for artists to live in?

Orwell's sins were different, but no less serious. They consisted in a persistent heterodoxy in relation to the basic assumptions made particularly by the Pragmatists about the working class and the Soviet Union. The condition of the working class in Britain, the behaviour of the Communist Party in Catalonia, were things that Orwell had seen with his own eyes, and he drew from his observations deeply irritating and embarrassing conclusions. So far had the rebels of the early Thirties hardened into orthodoxy that they regarded it as almost irrelevant to consider whether what Orwell said was true. They said that the eye of the individual was always myopic, that he saw a picture inevitably blurred and incomplete, and to more direct questioning they answered in that phrase of Day Lewis's which could be used to justify any murder or atrocity: 'Will the use of violence in this particular, concrete situation benefit the majority of persons concerned?' What we saw during the Thirties was an attempt to deny utterly the validity of individual knowledge and observation. So, when Spender asked his friend Chalmers what he thought about the 1938 Moscow Trials, in which Yagoda, who had been responsible for the investigation that led to the earlier trials, was himself sentenced to death, Chalmers asked calmly: 'What trials? I've given up thinking about such things long ago.'

Not many of the intelligentsia had grown so strong a carapace of unthought: but still, their attitude towards the Soviet Union, their belief in what was incredible and their savage treatment of unbelievers, was the blackest betrayal of their own integrity. One must make a distinction here. The impulse that prompted the intelligentsia to support the Spanish Republican cause, whether heroically or absurdly manifested, was a generous one. They could not be aware of the deceits practised upon them by the Koestlers, the Cockburn-Pitcairns and others, nor did most of them realize for some time that they were pawns, used deliberately not for Spanish but for Russian ends. But the impulse that led them to express faith in the Soviet Union after the Moscow Trials had no better motive than self-preservation. Twitch away this blanket of belief, and they would be left naked and shuddering to face the winter wind of reality. It would be pointless to put down in detail the monstrous incongruities that they willingly swallowed, pointless because these arguments have been rehearsed so many times, and also because they are arguments no longer. With the Nazi-Soviet pact of 1939 came the flight of the fellow-travellers, and this flight automatically reversed their verdict on the Moscow Trials, which now became obvious frame-ups. But they had not been deceived. In relation to the Soviet Union they had deceived themselves, and in the end one has to pay bitterly for such self-deceits.

The assault on the standards of the Thirties made by Robert Graves and his disciples was aesthetic, and not political. Graves himself showed always a marked dislike for the manifestation of political feeling in art, and professed to think himself ignored for that reason. 'My entry in the great Left Dossier is now something like this,' he wrote ironically. 'Graves, Robert. Sometime friend of Siegfried Sassoon, the Pacifist poet. His critical investigation of folk-rhythms heralds dawn of PROLVERS-TEK.' Graves's view was that Auden's poetry, and by extension that of his close followers, was wholly imitative, and worthless. The imitation, in Auden's case, was of Graves himself and of Laura Riding (if Auden was in fact his literary offspring, Graves once said, he was not prepared to legitimize the child), and Graves later committed himself to the view that Auden was a poet who had perhaps not written a single original line. I well remember going to dinner with a Gravesian who produced with some relish a copy of 'Spain' and suggested that we should prepare a line by line exegesis of the poem showing its multifold debts to Graves and other writers. My refusal, which was combined with some mildly critical references to Laura Riding, was not well received. Audenites were as unpopular in the Graves circle as Trotskyists at a Communist Party conference.

The poetic talent of the Auden Group was questioned by others as the decade advanced. The stirrings of revolt were subterranean, but real. *We are all romantics today*, yes, but some are more romantic than others, and a number of young writers found themselves uncomfortably confined both by Left wing orthodoxy and by the sharp discouragement of vague poetic feeling in *New Verse*. That *nauseating concern for poetry* was being felt again, and a new generation of writers had appeared above ground that was to take Dylan Thomas as poetic herald of a New Apocalypse, an acknowledgement which the herald accepted with pop-eyed surprise. Then there were many writers as yet little known, like C.P. Snow and his scientfic colleagues, who found the content of the proletarian work in *New Writing* trivial and the Audenesque jokes silly. There were devotees of the Twenties, like Anthony Powell, who once briskly said that he thought the work of the whole Auden Group worthless. There was Edith Sitwell, who dismissed Louis MacNeice's poems by saying that they were very dull and seemed to be covered in chocolate. The literary wars of the period were more spirited and more destructive than any conducted today; it may be worth recalling one of them, as an indication of – what? The resilience of literary reputation, perhaps.

In November 1934, G.W. Stonier reviewed in the *New Statesman* Edith Sitwell's book, *Aspects of Modern Poetry*. The book was, he said, very largely a defence of modern poetry against the Big Bad Wolf, Dr Leavis (whose opinion of Miss Sitwell's talents was known to be low). How odd it was, then, to find quite remarkable similarities between this book and Dr Leavis's own *New Bearings in Modern Poetry*, published a few years earlier.

'If the reader will compare Miss Sitwell's chapter on Yeats with Mr Leavis's remarks on the same poet, he will find that these two critics think more closely alike than Miss Sitwell's "attack" would seem to suggest. For example, Miss Sitwell begins by quoting Lang's sonnet, "The Odyssey"; this sonnet was quoted, with the same intention and effect, by Dr Leavis.'

Stonier went on to point out over a dozen cases in which the same passages had been quoted and very similar remarks made about them, and ended by saying that he preferred Dr Leavis. 'One never doubts his accuracy; Miss Sitwell's chapter on Hopkins contains numerous mistakes in quotations, beside misspelt names.'

The hunt was up. In the following week a correspondent gave a further nineteen parallel quotations in detail, and a week later Geoffrey Grigson discovered several parallels between Miss Sitwell and Herbert Read in their writings about Hopkins.

'Sprung rhythm is not an innovation; it is the rhythm natural to English verse before the Renaissance. It is the rhythm of *Piers Plowman* and of Skelton.'

Read

'We may see, therefore, that Sprung Rhythm is not an innovation. Indeed it is the rhythm of *Piers Plowman* and the rhythm of Skelton.'

Sitwell

At the same time Edith and Osbert Sitwell both wrote letters. Miss Sitwell said that had she known Dr Leavis was the author of the 'Odyssey' sonnet ('and I think him capable of it') she would have acknowledged her debt; Osbert Sitwell asked whether 'if I informed a class of school-children that the Normans invaded England in 1066 and if Dr Leavis had previously said the same thing, I should be guilty of plagiarising Dr Leavis?' Whether the use of Lang's 'Odyssey' as a starting point for considering the poems of Yeats is comparable to saying that the Normans invaded England in 1066 – that, it may be, is still in doubt.

'There are grounds to fear that strong tendencies are drawing some members of the "post-war" group away from the People's Front. *New Verse*, the periodical that has served as a major rallying-ground for them, has by now lost every semblance of a genuine Left wing journal.... It is systematically hounding Day Lewis for what it regards as an excess of Communist loyalty. It has every appearance of becoming a cesspool of all that is rejected by the healthy organism of the revolutionary movement – a sort of miniature literary Trotskyism.' So D.S. Mirsky in *International Literature*. The dread pejorative word, *Trotskyism*, had been spoken. As the Artists and Pragmatists became more dubious about Spain, Communism, Moscow Trials, so it became obviously the job of party-line stalwarts to keep back-sliders up to the mark. In reply Grigson said that *New Verse* had not meant to be a Left wing journal, although 'its editorial view of the nature of poetry is not idealist'. He added, with characteristic bloodthirstiness, 'The Berts of *Left Review* will certainly shoot the Cyrils and Raymonds of the *New Statesman*. We may clap at that; it will be small loss. But as the years pass they will shoot the Audens and the MacNeices and the Isherwoods', and that would be disastrous. It is interesting to notice that for the unpolitical Grigson, as for many others, 'Liberal' had become, like 'Fascist', a term of literary abuse. 'Mr Waley's fairly clean "Liberal" English seems much queerer and more lifeless than it did in 1918.'

'In all these skirmishes and ambuscades, movements backwards and sideways, barricades erected in England for the defence of Spain, totems worshipped and then put hurriedly away in the lumber room, struggles of form and content, psychology and politics, how, father, did you further the progressive cause? Come down off Mount Olympus and tell us.'

It is time, I suppose, to declare an interest. I may protest that today I am impartial, but of course that is not true (and I remember uneasily that *of course* was, at some time in the Thirties, excommunicated as Fascist English). The old political Adam shows himself, I am sure, in all sorts of assumptions. Looking out from whatever comparatively comfortable hidey-hole he has found in the lick-spittle Fifties, any denizen of the Thirties must be astonished by the targets in the sights of young Left wing artists nowadays. To draw a bead on the Establishment, on the Royal Family, on the antics of gossip column writers – are they really worth powder and shot? Should Kingsley Amis be quite so blandly happy in his adoption of an extremely anti-intellectual attitude, isn't the word *triviality* hanging ominously about?

> Quite often he was heard to babble
> 'Poets should be intelligible'
> Or 'What determines human fate
> Is the class structure of the state'
> Or 'Freud and Marx and Dickens found –
> And so do I – souls not profound.'

The sentiments are mine, although the words are those of my friend Roy Fuller. I present myself, then, as in some ways a standard Thirties model, in others a heretic. Standard items are age (b.1912), deep admiration of Auden's poetry and to a less extent of Auden-Isherwood plays, and the typical Thirties tendency to insist that works of art must be seen first of all as events in society, and yet to say that form and style are vitally important to an artist. But there are oddities which determined, and no doubt still determine, my attitude: non-public school, non-University, an outsider in relation to the Auden Group, editor of a verse magazine which introduced or gave a platform to some young poets also outside the Group. In another decade non-political perhaps, in this one entirely absorbed by the relationship of art and politics, distrustful of all Communist Party activities, for a few months a member of the Trotskyist Revolutionary Socialist Party. At the same time, to the indignation of many friends, an admirer of Wyndham Lewis.

> These times require a tongue that naked goes,
> Without more fuss than Dryden's or Defoe's.

I admired Lewis for the attitude expressed in lines like these, admired him as an artist in words and paint, asserting by my admiration that an artist's myth – the body of ideas that moves him to producing works of art – might be as politically reactionary as Lewis's. More than this, Lewis's couplet about himself seemed to me justified; he was, I thought, a corrective to the general Left wing orthodoxy. It is typical of my thinking that I should not even have contemplated the possibility of any *liberal* corrective of this kind. I was led at times into desperately extreme positions, and dutifully pick one of the worst horrors out of my personal junkheap. It comes from a review of Kenneth Allott's poems.

> Mr Allott is very careful about society ('I do not know much about society'), but one cannot be careful or modest enough....

It is all very well to say that this is the 'detached viewpoint', implies the reticence, etc., which is necessary for the artist *sometimes* (you pick your own times): the 'detached viewpoint' today is too near the mud-brained Liberal-Labour viewpoint, in poetry as well as politics. Better the *BU Quarterly* than the *New Statesman*, no readers at all than Plain Readers.

How can anybody have been so stupid, so insensitive, as to write such words in 1938? How could anybody think that the *British Union Quarterly* was in any way preferable to the *New Statesman*? In a sense these questions are unanswerable, and I admit the stupidity and the insensitiveness: but it is true also that those who condemn readily, without considering the social pressures that made otherwise intelligent people write such things, can never understand the Thirties. It was only a couple of years earlier, after all, that Harold Nicolson welcomed *One's Company* with the hope that Peter Fleming might become 'our' Horst Wessel. But my objective is not self-defence through attack on others. 'I don't defend my conduct, I explain it.'

To be as heretical as I was absolves one from feelings of guilt. It is the orthodox who feel guilty when the ground of their belief is taken away and it was the orthodox fellow-travellers, not Communist true believers or heretics, who turned to the consolations of psychology and symbolism.

It always seemed to me that Marxist materialism was absolutely irreconcilable with Freudian psychology, and I read with thorough approval John Strachey's scornful reference to Freud as 'one of the last great theorists of the European capitalist class' in *The Coming Struggle For Power*, and the criticism in *Left Review* which pointed out that the conclusions of psycho-analysis were largely drawn from a limited section of the leisured and cultured, and that 'Freud might never have heard of the fact that the human individual under Western civilization is a member of a class.' But any idea which in any period seems to correspond with a personal apprehension of reality will be rationalized so that it can co-exist with other and perhaps contradictory ideas. Thus, the materialist view of society presented by Strachey corresponded for many people with what they saw happening around them, but the psychological view of it derived from Freud corresponded very directly to what they felt in their own natures. Those

who regarded themselves as both Freudians and social materialists
had therefore a double set of values. They assessed their own
behaviour and that of their friends by psychological tenets, while
applying Marxist ideas to all mass social movements. It was inevitable
that this should happen, for to say that Hitler was a psychopatholog-
ical personality of a compulsive and sadistic type was of no help at
all in discovering how to get rid of him. Some of the politicians decided
that psychology had its subsidiary uses. John Strachey, in writing of
a book called *Freud and Marx*, forgot that Freud was a theorist of the
capitalist class:

> He (the author) shows that while Trotskyism, like fascism, is,
> of course, basically a political and economic phenomenon, yet one
> cannot exhaustively explain it without recourse to modern psycho-
> logical knowledge. Above all one cannot guard against the recur-
> rence of this terrible disease of degeneracy, to which men and
> women either within, or, more often, just on the fringes of the
> working class parties, have shown themselves subject, without
> recourse to psychological knowledge.

Must there not have been a blush on Strachey's cheek, must his
pen not for a moment have faltered, when many years later he expressed the view that Trotsky was a great and ill-used man? But this is
by the way. The Artists were not concerned with using psychology
to prove political points. Psychology gave them a wider ground for
expressing in art their feelings of guilt.

'Someone must have been telling lies about Joseph K, for without
having done anything wrong he was arrested one fine morning.' One
hardly needs to read further than the opening sentence of *The Trial*
to understand why Kafka exerted so much influence over English
prose writers in the late Thirties. Like Kafka's heroes they were aware
of guilt without being able clearly to discover its nature; like them,
were in rebellion against the authority which they respected, and to
which they desired to submit. 'If an authority is good why should it
not be feared?' K asks in *The Castle*, and this too was a question that
fellow-travelling artists asked themselves. Yet the opposite view
which may also be found in Kafka, 'All virtues are individual, all
vices social', was again, in a way, exactly what they felt. And the

working-out of the individual's struggle against authority with every possible complication and subtlety, the assertion of his code of values at the moment of their necessary and inevitable defeat, these things appealed to the deepest elements in their natures. I avoid, out of personal distaste for them, the obvious psychological interpretations, and say only that, like Kafka, these writers were unable to fulfil their longing for submission to an impersonal force.

Kafka's influence did not spring solely from the fact that artists in the Thirties were able to identify his moral problems with their own, but also from the evident possibility of applying his symbolism to the social situation. Malraux and Hemingway had been able to say something directly about the social and moral problems of the time without using symbolism or descending to propaganda, but this direct approach was (as it seemed) possible because they were both men of action. The symbolism of Kafka offered another strategy to those who were not eager participants in warfare. The artists might tell the truth of our times symbolically or in parable. I remember going round, after first reading Kafka, telling my friends that his apparatus of ambiguity could be used for all sorts of purposes, comic, tragic or merely mysterious, and that such a technique might produce anti-Fascist fairy tales of great power and beauty.

'Can one ever, I wonder, be quite at ease this side of the frontier?' The question is asked of the idealist philosopher Don Antonio by the valiant hero George in Rex Warner's *The Wild Goose Chase*, the only really effective book written in this form, although something of the same use of symbol and allegory can be seen in Edward Upward's *Journey To The Border* and Ruthven Todd's *Over the Mountain*, in which the hero who thinks that he has crossed the mountain and found a Fascist state on the other side discovers at the book's end that he has all the while been in his own country. Warner's master here was less Kafka than Bunyan, but it is a Bunyan who turns the horror of the time to comedy. So the ruthlessness and viciousness of the police is lessened by their crystal helmets, straw truncheons and continual idiotic grins, which give them some resemblance to the toy policemen in Beatrix Potter. The Rev Hamlet, the priest who tries to turn the revolutionary party to the uses of the Government, and carries a cylinder of poison gas beneath his cassock, speaks in the language of farce, with a Mortmere intonation. ('Look here, you fellows, I want you to treat me just like one of yourselves.... I'm not one of those stiff dry-as-dust parsons, who are always telling you what not to do. I want us all to get together and have just as jolly a time as we possibly can have.') The caricature of Mosley is conceived in purely comic terms ('My policy is a policy of Action, a policy of virility. The time has come to do away with every idea which is not vital in the most vital sense of that word'), and so is the celebrated football match (rugby and not soccer, of course) in which the victory of the Cons is announced in advance, and in which George's desperate efforts as referee to see that the game is played fairly are ended by the Cons mowing down the Pros with machine guns. But I don't want to criticize *The Wild Goose Chase* from a specifically literary point of view, but only to show that the use of allegory and symbolism did not in any way solve the problem of communication. The would-be followers of Kafka and Bunyan still wrote and thought in terms of Mortmere and public school, they still (with the honourable exception of Spender) made no attempt to treat Fascism as anything but a subject for farce, they remained still on their own side of the frontier, not quite at ease.

Munich. Louis MacNeice is a wonderfully sensitive recorder of those weeks in his long poem *Autumn Journal*, expressing almost perfectly the feelings of the most intelligent members of the Audience; yet the emotion he records here, the appalled sense that a way of life was over, did not last.

> Hitler yells on the wireless
>   The night is damp and still
> And I hear dull blows on wood outside my window;
>   They are cutting down the trees on Primrose Hill.
> The wood is white like the roast flesh of chicken,
>   Each tree falling like a closing fan;
> They want the crest of this hill for anti-aircraft,
>   The guns will take the view
> And searchlights probe the heavens for bacilli
>   With narrow wands of blue.
> And the rain came on as I watched the territorials
>   Sawing and chopping and pulling on ropes like a team
> In a village tug-of-war; and I found my dog had vanished

And thought 'This is the end of the old régime,'
But found the police had got her at St John's Wood station
And fetched her in the rain and went for a cup
Of coffee to an all-night shelter and heard a taxi-driver
Say 'It turns me up
When I see these soldiers in lorries' – rumble of tumbrils
Drum in the trees
Breaking the eardrums of the ravished dryads –
It turns.me up; a coffee, please.

What one has to remember always in thinking of a period, and what one can never quite convey in writing about it, is that things bear quite a different appearance at the time to the artificial historian's neatness that is imposed upon them afterwards. What Munich showed to many people was the need to prepare for war; but many others, including Left wing politicians like James Maxton and Fenner Brockway, thanked Chamberlain for preserving peace, and hoped that the peace might be permanent because the alternative was so terrible to contemplate; and to supporters of the Popular Front, Munich was merely one more proof of the need for collective security, something that they took metaphorically in their stride. Their reaction was neither to wish for British rearmament nor to thank Chamberlain; it was rather to feel that although war would have been terrible, peace on such terms was even worse.

But once again
The crisis is put off and things look better
And we feel negotiation is not vain –
Save my skin and damn my conscience.
And negotiation wins,
If you can call it winning,
And here we are – just as before – safe in our skins;
Glory to God for Munich.
And stocks go up and wrecks
Are salved and politicians' reputations
Go up like Jack-on-the-Beanstalk; only the Czechs
Go down and without fighting.

What was the whole affair but one further proof of what they had always maintained, that the Chamberlain Government would in the end give way to Hitler? It seems in retrospect that one likely effect of the Munich settlement might have been a decrease in support of the Left Book Club, as its members saw that the Club had been powerless to influence events in any degree; but this was not at all the case. On the contrary, it made liberal sceptics like MacNeice believe for the first time that collective action was essential, and that they must participate in it.

> For from now on
>   Each occasion must be used, however trivial,
> To rally the ranks of those whose chance will soon be gone
>   For even guerrilla warfare.
> The nicest people in England have always been the least
>   Apt to solidarity or alignment
> But all of them must now align against the beast
>   That prowls at every door and barks in every headline.

The Left Book Club never approached the figure of a hundred thousand members that had been prophesied in the early months, but the membership rose slowly until it topped sixty thousand, and Munich had no significant effect upon the graph of its rise. It is true that Victor Gollancz, many years afterwards, found himself looking again at the Club's activities and saw 'something rather wicked' about it, mixed up with a great deal that was good: an element of Hitlerism, almost, in reverse', but this is a late gloss, and at the time Gollancz said nothing stronger than that 'in my view the publications of the Club have tended to concentrate overmuch (though by no means exclusively) on two or three points of view, and to forget that any author has a place in our ranks, provided only that his work is of value in the struggle for peace and a better social and economic order and against Fascism.' This, however, had no effect at all on the books chosen, nor did Gollancz feel at the time that the Club was the wrong vehicle for expressing his ideas. The discussion groups continued their activities with undiminished zeal, and the Labour Party became increasingly anxious about the political use of these groups. Herbert Morrison said that

> There is ample evidence that the Left Book Club movement, through its groups, has become a political movement with substantial money behind it, and that one of its main activities is in the

direction of manipulating and controlling local Labour parties. This cannot be tolerated.

The biggest Left Book Club meeting of all was to come, when in April 1939, thousands attended a rally at the Empress Stadium, Earl's Court, which was addressed by Lloyd George, Sir Stafford Cripps (recently expelled from the Labour Party because he refused to stop advocating Popular Front policies) and the Liberal Sir Norman Angell, as well as by Pollitt and Ellen Wilkinson, who defied an official Labour Party edict that she must not speak upon the same platform as the excommunicated Cripps. It was the greatest triumph of verbal collective security (should one call it?) that Lloyd George and Norman Angell should have been persuaded to speak upon the same platform as Pollitt and Cripps.

The extraordinary obliviousness of reality (as it seems today) shown by the Popular Front's supporters can be understood by considering the confused blur of togetherness in which things happen. In September 1938, the issue of the Spanish Civil War was still undecided, and when Popular Front supporters talked about Munich they were thinking, as often as not, about Spain. To the general rule that we really apprehend only the political events that directly affect our personal lives there are some exceptions, and the most notable exception in modern times is the way in which the intelligentsia clung to the belief that the Spanish Republican cause in Spain must win finally to victory. Almost the only gesture of optimism in MacNeice's *Autumn Journal* concerns a return to Spain, which he had previously visited as a tourist. Spain is contrasted in the poem with French cynicism and British indifference; Spain is, it would not be much of an exaggeration to say, some sort of compensation for Munich, and if victory can be won there it may still affect the whole course of European events.

> The road ran downhill into Spain,
>   The wind blew fresh on bamboo grasses,
> The white plane-trees were bone-naked
>   And the issues plain:
> We have come to a place in space where shortly
>   All of us may be forced to camp in time:
> The slender searchlights climb,
>   Our sins will find us out, even our sins of omission.

When I reached the town it was dark,
   No lights in the streets but two and a half millions
Of people in circulation
   Condemned like the beasts in the ark
With nothing but water around them:
   Will there ever be a green tree or a rock that is dry?
The shops are empty and in Barceloneta the eye-
   Sockets of the houses are empty.
But still they manage to laugh
   Though they have no eggs, no milk, no fish, no fruit, no tobacco,
      no butter,
Though they live upon lentils and sleep in the Metro,
   Though the old order is gone and the golden calf
Of Catalan industry shattered;
   The human values remain, purged in the fire,
And it appears that every man's desire
   Is life rather than victuals.
Life being more, it seems, than merely the bare
   Permission to keep alive and receive orders....

I have loved defeat and sloth,
   The tawdry halo of the idle martyr;
I have thrown away the roots of will and conscience,
   Now I must look for both,
Not any longer act among the cushions
   The Dying Gaul;
Soon or late the delights of self-pity must pall
   And the fun of cursing the wicked
World into which we were born
   And the cynical admission of frustration
('Our loves are not full measure,
   There are blights and rooks on the corn').
Rather for any measure so far given
   Let us be glad
Nor wait on purpose to be wisely sad
   When doing nothing we find we have gained nothing.
For here and now the new valkyries ride
   The Spanish constellations
As over the Plaza Cataluna
   Orion lolls on his side;

Droning over from Majorca
  To maim or blind or kill
The bearers of the living will,
  The stubborn heirs of freedom
Whose matter-of-fact faith and courage shame
  Our niggling equivocations –
We who play for safety,
  A safety only in name.
Whereas these people contain truth, whatever
  Their nominal facade.
Listen: a whirr, a challenge, an aubade –
  It is the cock crowing in Barcelona.

One must see a double, and contradictory, process working in the Audience during these last years of the Thirties. To one side many of the Pragmatists and Artists were acknowledging with infinite reluctance the extent and nature of the deception in which they had willingly acquiesced, and were moving slowly away from all political attachments towards the point of view put forward by E.M. Forster, in *What I Believe*. Tolerance, good temper and sympathy, Forster said, were the prime virtues, personal relationships were at least 'comparatively solid, in a world full of violence and cruelty'. One should not give more than two cheers even for Democracy.

  Democracy is not a Beloved Republic really, and never will be. But it is less hateful than other contemporary forms of government, and to that extent it deserves our support. It does start from the assumption that the individual is important, and that all types are needed to make a civilization. It does not divide its citizens into the bossers and the bossed – as an efficiency-regime tends to do. The people I admire most are those who are sensitive and want to create something or discover something, and do not see life in terms of power, and such people get more of a chance under democracy than elsewhere. They found religions, great or small, or they produce literature and art, or they do disinterested scientific research, or they may be what is called 'ordinary people', who are creative in their private lives, bring up their children decently, for instance, or help their neighbours. All these people need to express themselves; they cannot do so unless society allows them liberty to do so, and the society which allows them most liberty is a democracy.

It was towards such a political quietism, and away from belief in the Age of Faith ('It is extremely unpleasant really. It is bloody in every sense of the word') that one section of the Audience unconsciously moved. To this attitude there was counterposed that of anti-Forsterian liberals like MacNeice who felt that they had lived too much in the world of personal relationships, and that Fascism presented a threat before which all individualism must seem finicky. These reluctant recruits to the idea of collective security were not really an adequate replacement for those who were deserting the cause, but this was not apparent at the time.

These are public events. A private one, reported in the *Daily Express* of January 19, 1939, had more than a purely personal significance.

To USA, last night, to lecture and see about staging of their last play: poet Wystan H. Auden and collaborator Christopher Isherwood.

To this may be added a report in the *Evening Standard* a couple of months later.

The young pair are not wholly impressed with the New World. They shut themselves up in a flat in one of the city's less fashionable slum districts. Here, in conclave, they proceeded to evolve a new philosophy of life. Its main principle, I gather, is a negation of Auden's previous thesis that art is inseparable from politics.

14

The Dream Revolved

What people do, whether they prefer to live in England or America, is, in the simplest sense, obviously a matter for the people themselves, but the departure of Auden and Isherwood had a symbolic importance that was nothing to do with their personal lives. '*New Verse* came into existence because of Auden,' Grigson wrote in reviewing *Journey to a War*, and in a very real sense Auden's devices of style and habits of feeling *are* the Thirties, or a large part of the Thirties. That this marvellous monster of poetry and his coadjutor, the most sensitive prose writer of his generation, should be prepared for a lengthy exile in America, that there should be rumours of Isherwood's interest in. Yoga, that Auden should begin to produce work suggestive of an almost complete change of social attitude, all this deeply shocked admirers to whom it seemed something very much like desertion. The importance of their self-ordered exile does not rest at that. It has been said that Auden probably experienced some profound traumatic experience in Spain, and it does not seem very fanciful to suggest that after Munich Auden and Isherwood felt ('felt' rather than 'thought') that, whatever might happen, their Europe, the Europe from which they had drawn artistic life, Berlin at the end of the Twenties, Austria before Hitler, Spain, the Popular Front in Britain – was dead. Their departure to America may best be seen as an act of artistic prescience, away from the unrewarding world of ARP and BBC, fire fighting and square bashing, in which the poets who stayed were soon to be immersed. To talk about cowardice is absurdly beside the point; to question the final artistic wisdom of the step they took is another matter. It is possible that, had they stayed, the Thirties movement might have had a less ignominious end, possible also that they might have found some artistic sustenance in wartime Britain.

In December 1938, all that was left of the British battalion of the International Brigade returned from Spain. The Brigade had been disbanded at the request of the Spanish Repubican Government, in the faint hope that its voluntary withdrawal might somehow induce the withdrawal of the thousands of Italian troops who were fighting for Franco. They came into Newhaven singing, with the flag of the Spanish Republic waving from the ship, and beside it the Major Attlee banner in red and gold, which Attlee had personally presented to them. At Victoria Station the 309 men were led out by three of their wounded, one hobbling on crutches. Their reception committee included Attlee, Cripps, Norman Angell, Will Lawther and Lord Strabolgi. 'We are proud of you,' Attlee said. 'You have stood for the cause of the workers.'

A great celebratory meeting was held at Earl's Court, attended by more than nine thousand people. 'The Battalion disperses, not for all time,' said the announcer. 'On the call of freedom once again they will parade. Wherever democracy is threatened, they will march again to its defence.' And Harry Pollitt: 'We yield to no one in our confidence of the ultimate victory of the Spanish Republic.'

While these speeches were being made, Franco's Italians were already driving towards Barcelona. Within a fortnight the city had fallen, and two months later the defence of Madrid was abandoned. George Barker's 'Elegy on Spain', from which I take the last three verses, seems to me the most moving poem written about the struggle.

> Farewell for a day my phoenix who leaves ashes
> Flashing on the Guernica tree and Guadalajara range.
> Change is the ringing of all bells of evil,
> Good is a constant that now lies in your keeping
> Sleeping in the cemeteries of the fallen, who,
> True as a circling star will soon return
> Burning the dark with five tails of anger.
>
> What is there not in the air any longer,
> Stronger than songs or roses, and greater
> Than those who create it, a nation
> Manhandling god for its freedom: lost,
> O my ghost, the first fall, but not lost
> The will to liberty which shall have liberty
> At the long last.
>
> So close a moment that long open eye,
> Fly the flag low, and fold over those hands

Cramped to a gun; gather the child's remains
Staining the wall and cluttering the drains;
Troop down the red to the black and the brown;
Go homeward with tears to water the ground.
All this builds a bigger plinth for glory,
Story on story, on which triumph shall be found.

But rhetoric can be justified only by success. It was not merely the
first fall that had been lost. As an event in history, and as a symbol
of hope, pride and reproach for the intelligentsia, the war was over.

> The Cabinet plan to provide work for many thousands of
> unemployed in digging ARP trenches in towns all over Britain.
> The work will be paid for at the usual rates.
>
> *Daily Express*, 4 November 1938

Everybody with the faintest trace of sensibility felt in those last months
before the war that something was over: and that 'something' was
not just the end of peace and the coming of war. It was rather that
a whole way of life was over, that some terrible worm had been at
work eating away individual generosity and idealism, and secreting
in their place brutal cynicism and self-satisfaction.

A tiny illustration of the sort of thing I mean is afforded, not by
any individual actions, but by the activities of the National Unemployed Workers Movement.

On December 21, 1938, forty unemployed men lay down in Oxford
Circus, and stopped the traffic. Their bodies were covered with slogans, and as fast as the police picked up the men and took them to
the pavement, other men replaced them. This well-organized
demonstration held up traffic for the best part of an hour.

On the following day fifty unemployed workers walked into the
Ritz and asked for tea. They took a wrong turning, and found themselves in the Grill Room instead of the Tea Lounge.

> Upstairs in the lounge the five-piece band went on playing their
> In-a-Persian-Garden sort of music. The tea trolley was covered
> with sandwiches of smoked salmon, ham, pâté de foie gras, peach
> and raspberry fluffy pastries, cream sponge cakes, brandy snaps,
> meringues, and, for those who could manage them, hearty-looking
> fruit cakes.

'We've got money to pay for tea,' the men said, and produced it from their pockets. The mistake they had made in going to the Grill Room, however, foiled the attempt to have tea. They did not know where the Tea Lounge was, and nobody told them. After half an hour's argument they left.

That was only the beginning. On Boxing Day a group of workless men sang mock carols outside the house of Lord Rushcliffe, chairman of the Unemployment Assistance Board. On New Year's Eve twelve men climbed the Monument and hung out a banner from the top of it, demanding winter relief, and on the same day some hundreds of unemployed carried a plain black coffin, bearing the words 'He did not get winter relief' down the Strand and thence to Piccadilly. They were dispersed by police charges. Two or three days later the coffin arrived at Downing Street in a big lorry. The demonstrators wished to deliver it to the Prime Minister. The police had been warned of their presence, and a farcical struggle ensued between the men who were trying to get the coffin out of the lorry and the policemen who were pushing it back over the tailboard. In Glasgow a week later a flag was seen to be flying over the Unemployment Assistance Board office: 'This is the office of the UAB, which starves men, women and children.' A couple of days after that, men were found to have chained themselves to the railings outside Labour Exchanges. They carried placards saying: 'Release Us From Hunger.' In February a group of unemployed men burst into the foyer of Grosvenor House where Sir John Anderson, who was in charge of ARP preparations, was attending the Allied Brewery Trades Dinner, lay down on the floor covered with posters, and chanted 'We Want Work on ARP.'

A few of the recently-returned International Brigade were involved in these incidents. Lady Winterton spoke for a large part of the Conservative Party when she said: 'It is a pity that men who come home unemployed and make a nuisance of themselves with coffins and by chaining themselves to railings were not shot in Spain.'

The sympathy of the crowd was for the most part with the demonstrators, and all this, it may be said, was effective propaganda for the cause of the unemployed. But there was an enormous gap between the feeling that had inspired the hunger marches of 1936 and these demonstrations. The hunger marches were partly Communist-organized and Communist-led, but the men who marched from Jarrow carried with them the pain of a town and displayed the raw wounds of a nation. The dignity that they showed under hardship was a deep reproach to the well-fed, and the emotional effect of the marches far transcended their propagandist intention. The demonstrations of early 1939, on the other hand, were nothing more than well-organized stunts. Telephone calls to newspapers made well in advance ensured a big press, and although no doubt the demonstrators were out of work, the same faces were to be seen time and again, lying down in the streets or chained to railings, so that taking part in the stunts became for some of them a kind of job. The human drama of the Jarrow march had turned in the demonstrations before the war to cynically effective farce.

The Thirties movement died silently, without bang or whimper. The last issue of *New Verse* was that of May 1939, in which Grigson praised Auden as 'something good and creative in European life in a time of the very greatest evil', at a time when Auden was ceasing to be part of Europe in any way. The final issue of my own magazine, *Twentieth Century Verse*, appeared at about the same time. Both magazines ceased rather than ended, and the Group Theatre also ceased its activities when war came, the artistic impulse behind it extinguished now that Auden and Isherwood had gone. All was changed: no more poems about Spain, no more verse plays about the decay within a class of society or the problems of high-minded judges, no more anti-Fascist fairy tales in the form of novels, no more agonizing about Munich. By the end of 1939 the great tide of Left wing feeling had receded beyond the bounds of vision, and the land it had covered was as smooth, almost, as though the tide had never been.

Of the Thirties periodicals only *New Writing*, edited by the indomitable John Lehmann, survived, and in the end flourished, with its Penguin extension selling 80,000 copies of each issue. Unity Theatre also survived, presenting one of its most successful productions, Geoffrey Parsons's and Berkeley Fase's *Babes In The Wood*, in the months after Munich. In this 'Pantomime With Political Point', Chamberlain was the Wicked Uncle, and Hitler and Mussolini the Robbers. Several of the songs were recorded by Decca, and the pantomime was greeted with a chorus of praise from *The Times* ('irresistibly funny') to the *Daily Worker* ('I might advocate a couple more inches off the chorus girls' dresses'), with only Miss Eileen Ascroft in the *Daily Mirror* dissenting ('It was unfair and quite disgusting. I as a worker of Britain protest that such a show could be put on at the "Workers Theatre" ').

The Observer, in a half-column of praise, complained only that 'the sentiment of the songs seemed a thought doctrinaire'.

> Our sentiment is sympathetic
> To your society
> We need your aid
> In our crusade
> To work for Unity
> Together we'll build a land worth living in
> That's our policy
> To win the fight
> We must unite
> To work for Unity

Those who found themselves annoyed by such sentiments were still amused by the Fairy Wish Fulfilment ('I'm the Fairy Wish Fulfilment, My best friend is Godfrey Winn'). The success of *Babes In The Wood* prompted ambitious plans to turn Unity into a professional company, and a lease was actually taken on a theatre in the West End. But the war put an end to these schemes, and Unity never again had the kind of success achieved by *Babes In The Wood*, which touched exactly a nerve of anti-Chamberlain feeling after Munich.

To those outside the Thirties movement at the time, and to some more recent commentators, it has appeared that its collapse was brought about by the declaration of war, but this is very much an over-simplification. We have seen Auden and Isherwood abdicating from responsibility months before the war began, we have seen the slow loss of faith among others in the Auden Group: and the two events that really broke the spirit of the movement, and destroyed among those who had led it their belief in the necessary interaction of art and politics, were the defeat of the Spanish Republic and the Nazi-Soviet pact. The first of these shattered the illusions nursed throughout the decade that history was on the side of democratic movements, and the second dealt a knockout blow to the many who had regarded the Soviet Union as the guardian of democratic institutions throughout the world, and as a source of permanent moral good.

The Left Book Club never recovered from the Nazi-Soviet pact. Gollancz and Laski supported the war that followed within weeks of it; Strachey opposed the war, and did not leave the Communist Party until the spring of 1940, when he decided that 'those controlling the

Daily Worker are prepared... to give way to Hitler to any extent, and
that they are utterly irresponsible as to the consequences to the British
people of such unlimited giving way.' So it was *national* feeling, after
all, that led to Strachey's disillusionment. He contributed to a book
called *The Betrayal of the Left*, edited by Gollancz. The activities of the
Communists were, Gollancz decided (to use the phrase that was suddenly no longer fashionable), objectively pro-Hitler. But to many
thousands of non-Communist Left Book Club supporters, the
attitudes of Gollancz, Laski and Strachey seemed a betrayal of
another kind. How, in the name of what was rational, could they
support the Government that they had been abusing for years? Wasn't
the attitude of Lloyd George, who wanted a negotiated peace, or
even the defeatism of the Communists, more logical? The Club's
members left in thousands. And as for the artists who had been at
the centre of the Popular Front movement, what was left to them
now but enlistment in some form of National Service, or (in the case
of the AIA) the attempt to induce the much-attacked Government
to employ artists on war work? They retained meanwhile the attitude
expressed by Day Lewis, months after the war had begun, in answer-
ing the question, 'Where Are The War Poets?'

> They who in panic or mere greed
> Enslaved religion, markets, laws,
> Borrow our language now and bid
> Us to speak up in freedom's cause.
>
> It is the logic of our times,
> No subject for immortal verse,
> That we who lived by honest dreams
> Defend the bad against the worse.

Revolving the dream once more, I am struck by one omission. 'You
have said that the artists were dreaming, you have told us the dream,
but you have not, except in the most politicized fragments, shown us
their art. Isn't this, after all, the only thing that matters?' Such a
criticism seems to me misconceived. To talk about the art as such,
to suggest the lines of development in Auden and Spender, to attempt
an assessment of the work produced through the AIA, would mean
engaging in the sort of criticism that I have tried to avoid. My object

has been to show how in this decade life affected art, to indicate the social forces and occasions which made artists work as they did. Extracts from poems, novels, essays have been chosen with that end in view. It may be possible, though, to make some cautious suggestions, far from definitive opinions, about the nature of the whole movement and the effect of politics on art in the decade.

It was, first of all, a poetic movement more than anything else, and this was partly because Auden printed his personality so firmly upon these ten years, and partly because the uplift of spirit in the early Thirties found expression most easily in poetry. And next, it was a bourgeois movement, in the sense that its most talented adherents had gone to public schools and fashionable Universities and that they brought into their work the language and attitudes derived from their backgrounds. It is the work of these writers that remains; the chunks of proletarian life presented with such enthusiasm by *Left Review* and later by *New Writing*, the stories and novels by miners and tool-makers and builders' labourers, are today utterly dead. Nevertheless, the bourgeois writers cast frequent longing glances at these genuine proletarians. The appeal of their own work was limited: wishing to speak as straightforwardly as Wordsworth, they found themselves talking in a language fully understood only by friends. As the Thirties passed they tried to reach a larger audience by writing novels, or plays in verse, or by blending verse with prose in such sugarcoated social pills as *Letters From Iceland*. *Only connect*: but always with the desire to communicate went the contrary wish to preserve the precious seed of individuality. 'Our hopes were set still on the spy's career, Praising the glasses and the old felt hat,' and they remained so throughout the decade.

Yet this adherence to private images and symbols was not only flippant or sensational. It rested in a belief that any attempt to express human relationships in art demands subtlety and complexity, and that the best art of our century had been subtle rather than simple. The art of the Thirties sprang from the tension between such a belief and the public events that seemed to deny it. The best art of our century might be complex, but what 'the age demanded' was simplicity, the direct speech of man to man. Could one really weigh the artist's inclination towards subtleties of thought and feeling with the duty to use his pen in support of social justice?

From this wet island of birds and chimneys
Who can watch suffering Europe and not be angry?
For death can hardly be ridiculous,
And the busking hysteria of our rulers,
Which seemed so funny to our fathers,
    Dirties the newsreel for us.

                                        Kenneth Allott

What can we do? The walls all round
Go four feet deep into the ground.
    But still, we have our pens;
Let this, by writing, be our purpose:
Distract the naturalist from his porpoise,
    The farmer from his hens,

To bring to those in mental attics
More than the facts of hydrostatics,
    A creed, a living thing.

                                        Gavin Ewart

'All virtues are individual, all vices social,' yet social action, class
action, mass action, is the duty of mankind: from these irreconcilable
propositions the best of the Thirties writers and painters made art.
This was a dilemma of a particular time and place, and it permitted
no evasions. Those who tried to solve the problem by subordinating
their art entirely to political feeling became Communist Party helots,
or like Edgell Rickword found themselves subdued to silence, or like
Day Lewis produced inferior work. Those who ignored the problem
suffered also, in that their art became trivial or incomplete. Nor is it
relevant to say that artists in other periods have solved such problems
easily or have found them non-existent. The problems were not the
same, the social mechanism impelling the artists was not the same.
A poem like this one, written to me by Roy Fuller from Africa during
the war, expresses the problem most eloquently.

I thought of you and Clapham Common, and
That pub on Denmark Hill with the skittle board,
Cricket in Kent on trodden, sunlit sand,

And many other places and occupations
Which, in the years before the war,
Appeared to have a value above their stations.

What was it? The innocence of our lives and pastimes
Against the sinister boiling up of Europe,
The sense that every beer might be the last time?

Or was it the love and kindness of our circle –
The only good? Certainly Victoria
And Camberwell, piquet and Blackheath, treacle

Tart and roast venison and paper games,
Seemed then most curiously virtuous,
Like the life and style of darling Henry James;

And seem so still, I must admit, as I
Look back, in this land to which the war has sent me,
At you and them with an unprejudiced eye.

But no nostalgia, none. For we have come
In actual experience of once
Feared evil to recognize more good. The drum

No longer terrifies: we march behind,
Are bored and sad, and history, we think,
Can do no worse. The loving and the kind

Are not restricted to the group around
The chessmen, and the state takes care of that
Old, gnawing wish for action. Oddly, I found

Last week, in a little, ancient magazine,
Some of the crabbed, uncompromising verses
We used to write. I wonder what they mean,

And if they have any worth, or was that all
Used up in our silent pity for the age,
Our desperate private love, the very small,

Vain contributions to integrity?
All those obscure, strange poems had a use.
Their unsuccess was fitting, they left me

With nothing but technique to fight the war,
No ships or alleys to escape by, nothing
To do but try to write a different way.

Not different, really; not even our writing changes,
But history sometimes seems to fit us, like
Growing boys fill for a time the clothes of strangers.

And temporarily we are smart and undivided.
For me, that time is now, I ask myself
How long: and if we must go back, to faded

Blackheath, and poignant Camberwell, or worse:
The cowardice of only being loved,
Of solitary, consolatory verse?

You know the answer. It is in those books
That haunted us, and haunt us, like words
Prophetic and frightening, and in the looks

Of the pythoness; and in the many who now
Surround us, whose destiny is coiled with ours.
Pray that we never again make up the few.

Most of the conflicts of the decade are here, the contrast between
private feeling and public action, the desire to have the private life
with all its hesitancies and contradictions expunged by the impersonal
force of history, the wish to create works of art that would no longer
be difficult to understand. But in the end, I suppose, solutions to
such problems come only from within. The answers imposed during
the war were temporary, the product of a particular time and place.
History did not fit us for long; the secrets remain in the books.

Notes on Sources

A good many of the sources used in this book are indicated in the text. The remainder are listed below.

CHAPTER ONE

The quotation from W.H. Auden is from *Poems* (1930). The quotation from A.J.A. Symons is from his introduction to *An Anthology of Nineties Verse* (1928). The facts about unemployment pay are drawn from *Britain in the Nineteen Thirties*, by Noreen Branson and Margot Heinemann.

CHAPTER TWO

'We made all possible preparations' comes from W.H. Auden's *Poems* (1930); 'Consider these, for we have condemned them' from C. Day Lewis's *The Magnetic Mountain* (1933); 'And through the quads dogmatic words rang clear' will be found in *Letters From Iceland* (1937); 'Gain altitude, Auden' is from *The Magnetic Mountain*; the two lines from Charles Madge appeared in *New Country* (1933); 'You whom I gladly walk with, touch' comes from *Poems* and 'Beethameer, Beethameer, bully of *Britain*' from *The Orators* (1932); 'Scavenger barons and your jackal vassals' is from *The Magnetic Mountain*. The four following quotations from Auden are from *Poems, The Orators, Look, Stranger* (1936) and *The Orators* respectively. The extract from Edward Upward will be found in *New Country*.

CHAPTER THREE

'The clock strikes ten' comes from *Look, Stranger*. The quotation from Stephen Spender will be found in *The Old School* (1934), and so will the prose quotations from Auden and William Plomer. The quotation from Giles Romilly is taken from the book *Out Of Bounds* (1935).

CHAPTER FOUR

The four lines from Stephen Spender will be found in his *Poems* (1933).

CHAPTER FIVE

The Aldous Huxley quotations come from his pamphlet 'What Are You Going To Do About It?' (1936), and Day Lewis's from his reply, 'We Are Not Going To Do Nothing' (1936). The John Strachey extracts are from *The Coming Struggle For Power* (1932). The poem by Bernard Spencer was written in the Thirties, but appeared in book form in *Aegean Islands* (1946).

CHAPTER SIX

The quotation from Sir Percy Harris can be found in Hansard, and those from Ellen Wilkinson in her book, *The Town That Was Murdered* (1938). 'And now no path on which we move' is from *Look, Stranger*, and Auden's comment on the Gold Medal presentation from a newspaper report. Geoffrey Grigson's remarks about it come from *New Verse*. The extracts from John Lehmann, Jack Lindsay and Maurice Carpenter were printed in *Left Review*. Gavin Ewart's poem is from *Poems and Songs* (1938). The extract from Philip O'Connor was printed in *New Verse*. Louis MacNeice's 'Bagpipe Music' appeared in *The Earth Compels* (1938).

CHAPTER SEVEN

The six lines from Gavin Ewart are taken from his poem 'Phallus In Wonderland' which appeared in *New Verse*. The four lines from Day Lewis's sonnet were first printed in *Left Review*. The sonnet, slightly altered, appeared in his book, *A Time To Dance* (1935). Tom Wintringham's poem is from *Left Review*.

CHAPTER EIGHT

The quotations from Rupert Doone appeared in *New Verse*, and so did the retort from Geoffrey Grigson. Jack Lindsay's 'Salute the Soviet Union' was printed in the Unity Theatre broadsheet.

CHAPTER NINE

David Gascoyne's poem 'Baptism' was printed in *New Verse*, and the quotation from Charles Madge comes from the same source. J.B. Priestley's comment on Surrealism comes from a newspaper article. Kenneth Allott's poem appeared in *Poems* (1938). Anthony Blunt's observations about revolutionary painting come from *Left Review*.

CHAPTER TEN

The quotations from Victor Gollancz and Ivor Montagu appeared in *Left News*. Hugh Dalton's comment on the Left Book Club is taken from a newspaper interview.

CHAPTER ELEVEN

The Mass-Observation report, and Charles Madge's comment on it, come from *New Verse*, and so does the Oxford Collective Poem. Julian Trevelyan's remarks about Mass-Observation are to be found in his autobiography, *Indigo Days*.

CHAPTER TWELVE

The quotations from J.B. Priestley and Sir Francis Meynell are extracted from a contemporary pamphlet. William Rust's remarks appeared in his *History of the International Brigade* (1939), and Tom Wintringham's in *English Captain* (1939). The quotation from John Sommerfield is taken from *Left Review*. It appears, slightly changed, in his book *Volunteer In Spain* (1938). The remarks by George Orwell about life in Barcelona are from his *Homage To Catalonia* (1938). The quotation from Auden is taken from 'Spain', printed first as a pamphlet and then in *Another Time* (1940). Stephen Spender's account of his activities during the Spanish Civil War is paraphrased from his autobiography, *World Within World* (1954), and his earlier observations about the Writer's Congress appeared in *New Writing*. The account of Arthur Koestler in Spain is extracted from his autobiography, *The Invisible Writing* (1954), and the Claud Cockburn story from his book *Crossing The Line* (1958). Tom Wintringham's poem, 'Granien', is taken from *Poems For Spain* (1939).

CHAPTER THIRTEEN

The Gavin Ewart quotation appeared in *New Verse*, and so did Wyndham Lewis's remarks on Communism and Fascism. The views about the Thirties attributed to C.P. Snow and Anthony Powell were expressed in conversation. Edith Sitwell's remark about Louis MacNeice's poems was made in *Life and Letters Today*. The whole of the Stonier-Sitwell controversy will be found in the *New Statesman*. The quotation from Roy Fuller ('Quite often he was heard to babble') is from *Epitaphs and Occasions* (1949), and the two lines from Wyndham Lews are from *One-Way Song* (1934). My review of Kenneth Allott's poems appeared in *Twentieth Century Verse*. John Strachey's remarks about Trotsky may be found in *The Listener*. All of the Louis MacNeice quotations are from *Autumn Journal* (1939). Herbert Morrison's attack on the Left Book Club was made in a newspaper interview. E.M. Forster's pamphlet, 'What I Believe', was published in 1939.

CHAPTER FOURTEEN

George Barker's 'Elegy on Spain' will be found in *Lament and Triumph* (1940). John Strachey's expression of disillusionment with Communism was printed in the *New Statesman*. C. Day Lewis's poem, 'Where Are the War Poets' appeared in *Word Over All* (1943). 'From this wet island of birds and chimneys' is taken from Kenneth Allott's *Poems*, and 'What can we do? The walls all round' from Gavin Ewart's *Poems and Songs*.

POSTSCRIPT
THE THIRTIES AND THE NINETIES

1

A Man of the Thirties

'What does that mean, a man of the Thirties?' a younger writer asked, when I had pinned that label to my chest in the course of conversation. Was it anything more than a label, he asked, convenient but pointless, since to view artists and writers in terms of decades was purely arbitrary? In some periods, however, a group is moved by a common spirit and shares artistic and often social assumptions unknown or alien to those of an earlier or later generation. An insistence on the supremacy of art over life marked off the writers of the 1890s from other Victorians, and a contrary insistence on art's links to the society in which it is produced similarly marked off the 1930s. The only other decade in this century self-contained in something of the same way is the Sixties, when the assumption was made that the only interesting art exemplified an ideal unlimited freedom of thought and behaviour. Such beliefs separate the artists and writers of the Sixties as sharply as those of the Thirties as the Thirties writers were alien to the ideas of the Nineties.

What it means to be a man of the Thirties is implied in the body of this book, but may be usefully repeated here. It is to see art first of all in terms of the social conditions and morality that produce it, and to deny the existence of any divine afflatus although to admit its possible value as a myth-making illusion. It is precisely to reverse Archibald MacLeish's statement that 'A poem should not mean but be', by saying that the being is nothing unless it also means. A man of the Thirties would agree with Ruskin that a conception of social morality must lie behind the finest art, and would insist that the morality is not personal but social. It follows that a concern with politics is desirable, although not essential, for a serious writer. Such politics are not those of the bread-and-butter kind concerned with the loss or gain of parliamentary seats, or even with the replacement in power of Buffy by Cuffy or Duffy, but those that affect directly the fate of a nation or a group within it. One of the criticisms made of Dylan Thomas's poems in the Thirties was that they were too much concerned with the body and the emotions, even the poet's own body and emotions, written too little out of an awareness that the socially visible world exists.

Such tenets were abandoned by many of the principal writers within a few years of the decade ending. Auden, like Christina Rossetti, turned from man to God and denied any validity to the socially conscious attitudes from which he had written, even saying specifically that poetry makes nothing happen. Like Auden, Christopher Isherwood became disenchanted before World War II with 'the Popular Front, the party line, the anti-fascist struggle', and turned to the consolations of religion. Cecil Day Lewis similarly abandoned his stated Thirties view that the artist's business was 'to give the mass an imaginative picture of the world' as it was or could be, reflecting later that his youthful Communism had a religious quality, and that he had always been biased against intellectuals. And not long ago I heard Stephen Spender say positively that the political positions adopted by many writers in the Thirties, himself included, had damaged their work. Only Orwell affirmed the importance of the social impulse by saying that 'looking back through my work I see that it is invariably where I lacked a *political* purpose that I wrote lifeless books'.

I should make a similar affirmation. I am an unregenerate believer in the value of a social approach to art and literature. *Social* is a better word than *political* if the latter is narrowly interpreted, and if 'social' seems still to carry an implication of the writer as artisan or engineer, it might be called more cautiously an attitude based on common sense and rationality. Geoffrey Grigson put it succinctly in 1939 when he said a poet should be 'some one with a moral sense who is more than ever careful to convey the inner by the outer shape of things'.

It is through such a view of the relationship between art and life that a man of the Thirties looks at the iceberg of the Nineties looming, as I write, out of the mist.

2

The Reason for a P.S.

The Thirties was published in 1960, and reissued fifteen years later with a few very minor additions and deletions. Another fifteen years have seen the publication of many memoirs and biographies, scholars have investigated the major and minor figures of the period, Valentine Cunningham's very comprehensive *British Writers of the Thirties* has appeared. A personal view like this one may still retain a flavour lacking in purely factual or academic accounts, but some details are inaccurate, others inevitably not up-to-date, yet to reissue the book with changes and corrections silently made would have been implicitly dishonest, robbing the original work of any quality it possesses as a document of its time. It seems better, then, to leave the printed pages as they stand, a piece about the period written by a period piece, and keep corrections for this postscript.

There are things I regret about the form of the book. It was deliberately shaped as an anthology with comments, but I have often thought that the nature of Thirties' ideas and achievements could better have been shown by a more inclusive and impartial work like Holbrook Jackson's *The Eighteen Nineties*. Cunningham's survey, with all its merits, is not such a book. He has trawled so widely, and examined so attentively the tiniest minnows brought up in his net, that the meaning and achievements of the decade have in the end escaped him. In particular, he brings such an insistent irony into comparisons between the ideals and practice of the most important figures as to imply that their writing has no interest at all. Jackson did not make the mistake of comparing beliefs and hopes with achievement, and the Thirties still await a similarly even-handed survey. Bernard Bergonzi's *Reading the Thirties* and Samuel Hynes's *The Auden Generation* offer sympathetic views of the period, but they are limited in Bergonzi's case by a rather wide-eyed view of what he calls in an ironic but also wistful line 'the perilous freedom in the air beyond the pylons', in Hynes's by concentration on the Auden circle. My other principal regrets about *The Thirties* are that a proper determination to show the worst as well as the best writing in the decade should have been made manifest in so many examples, when half the number would have made the point as well, and that visual art should have been treated so superficially. To have ignored both abstract artists and the Euston Road group was inexcusable. They were a little outside the brief I gave myself, to which Surrealism and the social realism of the AIA were directly relevant, but so much the worse for the brief. Other deficiencies may be briefly noted. The comment that the Thirties might have been called the homosexual decade could have been elaborated. There was more to be said about the little magazines and about Mass Observation. I console myself with the thought that more extended views of such things would have changed the shape of the book, and any value it has is as a personal, deliberately impressionistic survey. Even if I had tried, I should probably not have been able to manage anything up to Holbrook Jackson.

3

Does a Better Society
Mean More Government?

The young men and women who questioned the form of their society in the Thirties, of whom those that called themselves the Prometheans were an advanced guard, did so in the belief that a better way of ordering things was possible. They were indignant about the inequities committed or condoned by the ruling National Government, and saw no chance of changing that Government except through an overturn of society, but it would never have occurred to them to question the need for the beneficial organizing power of the state. Their concern was less to break down barriers than to put them up in different places, and so to replace the vicious by the good society. Auden's vision of the building of the Just City contained an awareness that 'the earth obeys / The intelligent and evil till they die', but the Just City was not a place of total freedom, or how could it have been Just?

It must appear to any man of the Thirties that the decade after the end of World War II saw a slow attempt to create the Just City. (I remark parenthetically that these remarks apply only to Britain, and it is no doubt an indication of the insularity still obtaining in this island to contemplate the building of the Just City in a single country.) The progress was tortoise-like, yet a movement did take place towards equality of opportunity, limitation of individual wealth, and an ordered, equable society in which the extremes of poverty were avoided. The names of Prime Ministers changed, but neither Labour nor Tory party questioned the state's major role in the ordering of society, nor that this role was upon the whole benevolent. I mention in *The Thirties* the idea 'advanced at present' (that is, in the late Fifties) 'by lunatic theorists that railway and Post Office services should be restricted until they *are* self-supporting', and the absurdity of the idea would then have received general assent. The lunatic theorists have been in power for a decade now, and the decline of both rail and postal services is evident, but that is by the way. The point is that up to the end of the 1950s society in Britain did not change greatly from the shape it had taken in 1945 with the advent of the Labour Government, and that this orderly society crawling towards equality and accepting many limitations on social, business and personal freedom received general assent.

The change in attitude among the generation that became adult in the Sixties was radical, whether one dates it from 1960 (the year when the *Lady Chatterley* trial gave the freedom of print to the word *fuck*) or 1963 when sexual intercourse began, according to Philip Larkin, and the Beatles became famous. Its causes also can be variously attributed: to the fact that this was the first generation aware throughout their lives of the possible annihilation of civilization through nuclear war, the development of the contraceptive pill late in the decade, disillusionment with the deadening of ambition through the Welfare State, the rapid erosion of the need for human endeavour by technical advance in such diverse fields as car manufacture and television viewing, or to a medley of these things. Whatever the reasons, this was a rebel generation with utterly different aims and ideals from those of the rebels of the Thirties. Their revolt was international, and in some countries violent. In France students and their supporters nursed for a few days the illusion that their protest about the quality and conditions of teaching might cause the overthrow of the government. At New York's Columbia University in the same year of 1968 students claimed to have liberated the University, the black students condemning its white government as racist, and both black and white students agreeing that they should have the right to manage the University. Norman Mailer approved the uprising (which had counterparts elsewhere in the United States) as existential. Diana Trilling said more meaningfully that what happened at Columbia 'represented the disaffection from modern society and its authorities of people everywhere today'. The most extreme reaction was in West Germany, where the Baader-Meinhof group engaged in propaganda by the deed, the deeds being kidnapping, robbery and murder, the aim the destruction of the bourgeois state.

In Britain reactions were comparatively muted, perhaps because of the stability given to society by the Welfare State. Nothing comparable to the American troubles took place, although dissatisfaction with the forms and the nature of teaching was common, accompanied by questioning of the need for the existence of academic education.

This was strongest among students taking courses in the humanities, often doubtful that what they were studying had any relevance to the life around them. Those working in the sciences saw more readily the tangible worth of what they were learning. Although many students in Britain felt the intoxication of the challenge to authority posed by the Paris days, few can have thought anything similar was possible here, and there was nothing comparable to the Columbia students' stated intention to 'destroy *your* University', with its implication that 'our' replacement would be totally different.

In the end young people in the Sixties settled for 'disaffection from modern society' and not rebellion, although that was not the way they put or felt it. Yet the change from the Thirties attitude was almost total. Diana Trilling's idea of 'modern society' was very much that of Thirties rebels, a society ruled by reason and accepting the idea of order. It might be called a family with the wrong people in charge, as Orwell put it, but neither he nor any of the Thirties rebels contemplated the complete break-up of the family. That, however, was the end towards which rebels in the Sixties moved: not towards better government and, implicitly, an increase in state power, but towards destruction of such power and a vision of complete personal freedom. What I called thirty years ago the lunatic theorists, eager to dismantle all government-supported services and turn them into commercially profitable private enterprises, are nowadays fulfilling with nightmarish logic the implications of the demands made by the young in the Sixties. We offer you freedom to choose, lower taxes and more money to spend, the siren voices say, but the freedom to choose depends on the amount of money you possess, and the extra money in your pocket turns out to be fairy gold.

Such an outcome was not glimpsed by those who during the Sixties had felt themselves to be breaking social bonds regarded as inevitable restrictions by their parents and grandparents. The money in their pockets felt real enough, and was enough to buy the records and clothes they wanted. The Pill, and easy abortion if it failed, took the risk out of sexual coupling, and homosexuality was publicly acknowledged and became more popular now that it was no longer against the law for those over twenty-one. (The phrase 'sexual deviant', to be found in the preceding pages, would be named sexist in current cant, but is a statement of fact. While heterosexuality remains the norm, other practices are inevitably deviant.) The freedom of language brought by the *Lady Chatterley* decision was quickly used by some authors, while others refrained, and still refrain, from it. This freedom also worked its way into spoken language, which within a few years became noticeably more relaxed in sexual references, and also more violent. Violence was implicit even in the activities of those campaigning for peace under slogans like 'Make love, not war', and 'If it moves kiss it'. Freedom to drink and take drugs was also felt to be defensible, first on the ground that moderate drinking and the use of soft drugs was not harmful, with the fall-back line that any possible harm done was to the individual, and no concern of others. And the popular music of the time, whether that of the Beatles and their followers, or Bob Dylan and Joan Baez, had a note of simple exultation in physical pleasure, combined sometimes with the pseudo-religious feeling expressed in the phrase: 'We shall overcome'. In the Thirties Auden had used as epigraph for a book of poems: 'What can truth treasure, or heart bless, / But a narrow strictness?' That would have seemed an unintelligible question to many of the Sixties young, and those who understood would have found it deeply unsympathetic.

If it were said to me that in the Sixties the young were putting into practice the idea mentioned in *The Thirties* that 'experiment, in life as in art, seemed a vital necessity', and that 'the concept of "freedom" appeared an absolute good', my reply would be that the similarities were superficial, and that our idea of freedom was not the free-wheeling, anything-goes attitude of the Sixties, but one with social morality at its core. To say that the concept of freedom appeared an absolute good is not the same as a demand for absolute freedom. Some of the freedoms demanded and attained in the Thirties were foolish or self-negating, but they always had behind them the idea of the Just City, in which we should consent to the necessary limiting of individual freedom in the service of a virtuous strictness. Those who looked for freedom in the Sixties did so in the service of nothing at all except individual pleasure.

4

The Splintered Pyramid

The idea that British intellectual and artistic life took the form of a Pyramid, with a million-strong Audience at its base, Pragmatic worker bees above them, and the Artists at the top point (top in the sense that they were the producers of books, plays and paintings, the Pragmatists often explicators or commentators, the Audience the consumers) was relevant to the Thirties, but does not correspond to the present pattern of creation and consumption.

In half a century the Audience has changed almost out of recognition, and in changing splintered into separate and at time hostile groups. There is now what is called a black culture, a feminist movement, a homosexual literature in the service of which the word 'gay' has been appropriated. A backlash against all these movements has led to the coinage of the words *racist*, *sexist* and *élitist*. Both opposition to and support for the suppression of Salman Rushdie's *The Satanic Verses* is called racist; a woman writing to the *Guardian* calls for the banning of *Lady Chatterley's Lover* and attacks Lawrence as a sexist writer; anthologies of 'gay' stories are published with the suggestion that they have a qualitative difference from 'straight' stories. These and other splinters from the Pyramid make no acknowledgement of a common culture. They are not content to be part of a literary or artistic heritage but are consciously independent of it, searching back for examples that will provide a respectable historical background to black or feminist art. The splinters have less hostility to each other than to what they might still grudgingly acknowledge as the mainstream. A thesis on, say, *Black Gay Eighteenth Century Women Dramatists* might be warmly welcomed.

The concern of such groups is not with literature. Of course there are talented feminist novelists, Margaret Atwood and Doris Lessing among them, but within the group the feminism is the primary source of praise. The well-orchestrated hostility against the work of Kingsley and Martin Amis, the difficulty the first has in finding an American publisher, and the rejection of the second as candidate for more than one literary prize, rests on the fact that women editors and judges (perhaps some men too) have rejected their work as 'sexist'. Nobody has gone so far as to say outright that sexist writing can have no merit, since that would involve the dicey business of condemning a good many British, French and Russian classics, nor has anybody yet demanded that the work of either Amis should be banned, although no doubt many of its opponents are in the position of the man who detested Beardsley's drawings and wanted a short Act of Parliament to make that kind of thing illegal.

Sexist and racist are current cant, as today are fascist and democracy, labels of abuse or praise used instead of argument. They indicate how completely the nature of the Audience has changed. In the Thirties, the million who made it up (perhaps the number was an overestimate) shared a set of beliefs and common ideals, even if in practice they strayed from them. They 'believed sincerely that works of art were the fine flowers of a civilization whose proper glory was free speech'. The more ardent proponents of black, feminist and gay 'cultures' would find such a tenet at best an evasion, at worst racist, sexist or fascist in its implicit rejection of their work as something separate from and hostile to what they might call establishment writing.

The Audience has not only changed in its social and racial composition. Its belief in the basic virtue of art has been subjected to insistent moling attack on the part of the descendants of Thirties' Pragmatists, whose subterranean purpose has been to convince them that artistic standards do not exist. The sons and daughters of those past Pragmatists work for newspapers, television, colour magazines, record companies, and are dedicated to publicizing and praising what is fashionable, popular, or simply current news. A black candidate standing for the position of Oxford Professor of Poetry is news, so is a novelist who has lived for years on an otherwise uninhabited island, a sculptor who works only with bits of rusted iron, a painter who offers blown-up versions of comic cartoons, a television dramatist who replaces scripts by improvisation, a pop singer who insults his listeners or sends them into orgiastic ecstasies, a theatre director who puts Shakespeare into modern dress, adds bits of dialogue and introduces stage business. Phrases are invented that buttress the news value of such candidates for stardom, and make them look intellectually respectable. The television dramatist talks about the importance of the non-structured play and the theatre director about contemporary mores, art critics praise conceptual or performance art, the phrase *magical realism* is invented to describe fiction that blends reality with fantasy, poets insist on the importance of public performance, bits of old rubbish gathered together are said to symbolize a ruined Europe. The bewildered members of the Audience, anxious to be in the swim, dazzled by handsomely presented articles in the colour magazines and long articles by art critics and book reviewers, wonder: can this be art? Are comic postcards, pop songs, poems read as part of a stage show, art? The question would not be acceptable in those terms to the sociologists and socially-minded academics who are also among the descendants of those ancient Pragmatists, their response being *It is socially interesting*, or *This is popular culture*. They would not be conscious of evasion, for these are the terms in which they customarily think, but to anybody adhering to the beliefs of the Thirties they must seem a betrayal.

The gap yawning between the Thirties and the Nineties could not be better exemplified than in the different reactions to the idea of popular art. 'Art For The People' was a slogan of the Thirties, but the idea behind the slogan was that the Audience should be educated to a point at which they were capable of making distinctions between the shoddy and the subtle, the superficial and the profound, the enjoyable but trivial and the difficult but rewarding. The young Gavin Ewart put it lightly but well:

I should like to see
Better become best,
I should like to see the savage
Wear both shirt and vest.
I should like to see the daily press
Taking its views from the weekly reviews.

The attitude may be called condescending and arrogant, but it acknowledges and even demands acceptance of the existence of standards. The Nineties view of popular culture, however, is that if it's popular it *is* culture, and calls for study. The problem is to find out what kind of drama or literature the majority of people enjoy. Once discovered, this is called popular culture, a proper subject for the academic study that may fairly be called popular culture's end product. The fact that any form of popular culture may be the subject of articles in academic journals has the double effect of making it respectable, and through the respectability justifying the article.

An example close to my own experience shows the process at work. For many years the crime story was a critical Cinderella, condemned outright by Edmund Wilson, and praised by academics like A.J. Ayer only as a diverting relaxation, not to be considered in the same breath or on the same terms as a serious novel. In *Bloody Murder*, a history of the genre, I made a case for treating some crime writers, Dashiell Hammett and Patricia Highsmith among them, as novelists no less serious and interesting than many who are the subjects of long critical articles. That case has been accepted, but a concomitant of it was that distinctions were necessary between the tiny percentage of crime stories that had some literary quality, the much greater percentage that were entertaining and ingenious but trivial, and the great mass of ill-written rubbish. The making of such distinctions, however, and indeed the terms *judgement* and *literary value*, make those concerned with propagating and pushing popular culture shake as if with ague. Once admit that there are different levels of achievement in the crime story, and that at least ninety per cent of all writing in such forms as science fiction, the historical romance and the crime story is of no conceivable literary interest, and the whole basis of the present popular culture industry is destroyed.

In short, between those like me who want to show that some work done in a popular form can transcend the form's limitations, and those who applaud the form itself because a lot of people read, see or listen to it, there is no ground on which to meet. In the most recent edition of *Bloody Murder* I expressed dismay at what is happening, but while Sax Rohmer and Sexton Blake (among others) provide rich academic feeding grounds, no protests are likely to have much effect.

5

Real and Mock Revolution: is Warhol up to Shakespeare?

In 1917 Marcel Duchamp submitted to the Salon des Indépendants under the name of R. Mutt a marble lavatory bowl which he called 'Fountain'. A little later James Joyce ended an episode of *Ulysses* with a lengthy fart. Both were revolutionary gestures in the context of the beliefs and manners of the time. Duchamp's lavatory bowl was an insult to the taste of those who chose the pictures hung in the Salon, and also implied that a 'Ready Made', something manufactured in quantity, could be as much a work of art as easel pictures, which he saw as also mechanically made, more nearly duplicates of each other than original products of the imagination. The element of deliberate insult to the official art world was also powerfully present in the submission of 'Fountain', which of course was rejected. Joyce's literary fart, along with Bloom's orgasm, and later on the Nighttown scenes, were equally deliberate snooks cocked at authority. The language used and the actions described were both outside the limits of what could be put down on the printed page in Britain at that time. It is right to add that these were revolutionary *gestures* related to painting and literature, and that neither Duchamp or Joyce was a 'revolutionary' in the social sense.

Nevertheless what they did was offensive, and caused indignation. It was far removed from the literary and artistic pseudo-revolutions of the past fifty years, in which what were at the time Joyce's outrageous experiments with language and Duchamp's studied insults to the respectable have been used and abused for the edification of an Audience that, instead of being insulted, is delighted to be afforded the chance to participate in something *new*, even though the newness is an obvious illusion. For the novelty to be acceptable, it is necessary for a phrase like 'magical realism' to be accepted rather than defined, and for the art movements that succeed each other every decade to be taken unquestioningly into the corpus of art as truly fresh and interesting. The Audience looks to critics and reviewers for guidance, to see whether they should applaud the simplicities of popular art and minimalism, and the announced profundities of magical realism and near-photographic simulation of cartoons, but they look in vain, for critics refuse to make judgements of value.

A case presently to hand is that of critical reaction to the retrospective exhibition of Andy Warhol at New York's Museum of Modern Art and London's Hayward Gallery. Warhol is, one would suppose, the most obvious case of an artistic fraud perpetrated on the public, and of a reputation created by publicity. The single cinema shot of a man asleep lasting six hours, the shot of the Empire State Building extending the six hours to eight, the Campbell's soup tins indistinguishable except in scale from the real thing, the portraits of Marilyn Monroe, could anybody still be fooled into taking them seriously? It hardly seems to matter that Warhol's silk-screen works were often done by friends, who ordered the silk-screens, stretched the canvases, mopped on the paint, and then signed the result with the magic name.

But what was the reaction? In America if not reverential certainly solemn, in Britain questioning but again solemn. 'Is he a real artist or a jumped-up designer with pretensions?' Marina Vaizey asked herself in the *Sunday Times*, but that was a question she never answered, blending phrases like 'totally fascinating' and 'endlessly striking images' with others calling Warhol the master of hype and saying that 'consumerism is the dominant ethos' in his work and that 'it's the wrapping, not the content, that counts'. That can't be meant for praise, surely? Yet in a review that is a masterpiece of indecision, Vaizey concludes that the Warhol show is a knockout, and that he is 'the artist our society most deserves'. Like Christopher Hitchens in the *London Review of Books*, Vaizey mentions Duchamp, calling Warhol Duchamp's natural heir in a more solemn version of Hitchens's phrase that the French artist was Warhol's 'original Pop guru'. Neither writer makes reference to the different artistic and intellectual climates in which the outrageous has turned into the fashionable. Hitchens is delighted by the whole Warhol phenomenon, especially by what he calls the 'ad-man's gift for tags and phrases', the casualness about creating and signing canvases, and the fact that six 'shot-through Marilyns', punctured with bullets by a visitor to the studio, are now more valuable than the other Marilyn portraits. The *Independent* film critic calls 'Empire' the 'establishing shot to end all establishing shots', but seems to approve the immense length of this and other

Warhol films by calling them 'an extended meditation on the act of looking'. He is writing, we remind ourselves, of a single shot that lasts for several hours.

Such attempts to subtilise what should be briskly dismissed are not confined to Warhol. The *Independent* art critic Andrew Graham-Dixon, discussing the 'Conceptualist' art of Michael Craig-Martin, writes admiringly of 'An Oak-Tree', which consists of 'a glass of water on a glass shelf... accompanied by a text in which the artist asserts that what you are really looking at is an oak tree'. Conceptual art is the latest, or a recent, fashion. It means that an art work *is* whatever the artist calls it, no matter if it *looks* like something else altogether. I once invented a joke art movement called Immaterialism, the essence of which was that you painted only what was not there, and hence immaterial. Conceptualism is something like Immaterialism turned serious. The *Independent* critic looks at it with the straightest possible face:

> Isolating what it might take for a box or a glass of water to become art is a way of tackling the broader question... what is it, at base level, that art works do or are expected to do?

Very well. But what they are clearly not expected to do, except on the level of a conjuror's tricks, is to turn glasses of water into oak trees. The response such art demands is the modest one of 'What fun', not portentous remarks giving it the gloss of seriousness. Not that Michael Craig-Martin, all these years after the jokes of Duchamp, Picabia and others, sounds much like fun.

Such targets as Warhol and Craig-Martin may be thought too easy, not worth shooting down. That is not the case though, as the reactions I have quoted (there are many similar ones) make clear. There is an almost absolute critical refusal to make a distinction between what was historically revolutionary in style or subject (Duchamp, Cubism, Futurism, Vorticism, Suprematism in art; *Ulysses, Tarr*, early Eliot, early Stevens, early Faulkner in literature), and what is only fashionable or prompted by a desire to extinguish literature altogether like the late work of Beckett. There is also a refusal to acknowledge that standards of craftsmanship or style can exist.

The socio-philosophical implications of all this are, it should be repeated, of a levelling kind. If art is no more than a trick with mirrors (another Conceptualist ploy used by Craig-Martin), then the ingenuities of advertising and the trick effects obtained by photographers are art too. Such work creates no problems of appreciation for the Audience, since once the faculty of judgement has been suspended they feel free to give such cleverness something of the reverence they know it is appropriate to show in the presence of Rembrandt or El Greco. The levelling process is not overt but implicit – no critic would say Warhol's Marilyn was up to a Rembrandt portrait – but the implication is that they are to be regarded as in the same order of things. The Victorians knew differently, and better. They enjoyed the clever 'transparencies' by which one picture changed to another when held up to the light, a view of Greenwich Hospital turning into the Battle of Trafalgar, but did not regard them as more than amusing tricks. It is true that they revered Leighton and Alma-Tadema, a classical tradition of a bogus or decayed kind, but at least they made distinctions.

Of course the levelling process is not confined to easel pictures. Classic dramatists are mercilessly brought up to date. Chekhov is played with the minimum of scenery, when the atmosphere of the great plays is one of claustrophobic nineteenth-century convention demanding literal, photographic re-creation of Russian period settings; and almost every recent Shakespeare production contains ludicrous irrelevances. Pistol in *Henry IV* sports a Nazi swastika on his jacket, *The Merchant of Venice* is done in modern dress with the characters turned into City gents, *Macbeth* begins with the witches engaged in ballroom dancing on the blasted heath, Duncan is played by a woman who later appears as Macduff's son carrying a comic, one of Macbeth's officers is a woman in a flounced velvet dress.

Other contemporary versions of Shakespeare are less idiotic, but almost all have bits of purely modern stage business, accompanied often by patter meant to bring Elizabethan jokes up to date. The jarring nature of such innovations, and the damage they do the speaking of the verse and the nature of Shakespearean drama, is immense. Clever directors are led to such disastrous practices by, again, the need they feel to be popular and to put bums on seats. The aim is not to lift the Audience to appreciation of Chekhov's or Shakespeare's work as it was conceived, but to infuse the plays with material that ensures the Audience won't be bored. The results are almost invariably deplorable.

Such reflections are more apposite than they may seem to the opposition of Thirties and Nineties viewpoints. I have already apologized for some of my book's omissions, and a fuller survey of art in the decade would have revealed a social concern that extended well beyond the very literal realism of most of the AIA artists. Such concern marked the strictest abstract artists whose work flowered in the decade. It appears even in Mondrian, who believed that by keeping life out of his pictures altogether he could achieve through 'the horizontal-vertical division of the rectangle... [a] balance of the dualism [between] the universe and the individual'. This was essentially a social stance, in which the artist asserted that the lines and blocks of which his pictures were composed had a meaning beyond themselves. Mondrian, Moholy-Nagy, Ben Nicholson, Barbara Hepworth, Henry Moore and others would not have said they were making social points in their work, but they made no concessions to public taste of the kind found in Warhol, Lichtenstein, early Hockney and other Pop artists. (Although *concessions* is not quite the word, because the Pop artists of the Sixties and later were trying to *express* public taste.) In the Thirties the creation of art works, whether 'understood' or not, was the important thing, while for the Pop artist art is inseparable from public acclaim. And Thirties social feeling, which might be called social puritanism, could be found also in other arts, in architecture via all those who tried to fulfil the principles of Le Corbusier. The achievement of Le Corbusier, the young John Summerson said, was to have reconstructed current ideas about building forms, so that 'not a vestige of cliché remains in his designs... the machine, scientific building, mass-production, these are Le Corbusier's anchors to the world of commonsense, while he explores the underworld of form'. Le Corbusier was working, like the abstract artists, for a very small group and not at all to the popular taste of the time, which on its lowest commercial level was for ribbon development, on a higher income plane for mock-Tudor housing with bay windows and a pantiled roof. It is not important to the argument that Le Corbusier is now out of fashion, his ideas and in particular the execution of them derided. The point I am making is the difference in attitude between the Thirties and the Nineties. Le Corbusier too wanted to build the Just City. Architects now, having passed through a phase of distorting his ideas and making a botch of imitating his practice, are content with what is commercially acceptable, like the toy-town architecture of London's docklands, or such deliberately outrageous publicity-conscious works as the Pompidou Centre.

6

The Use of Politics

It is not surprising that the works of the Thirties that have worn least well are the Auden and Isherwood plays that, along with work by Eliot, Stephen Spender and Louis MacNeice, seemed at the time to offer hope of the revival of verse drama. How can one ever have thought that this was so? Reading the plays again I was shocked by the triviality of *The Dog Beneath The Skin* and the elementary Freudianism of *The Ascent of F.6* (Donald Davie's jeer at the 'craze / For showing Hector was a mother's boy' has a deadly accuracy), while the worthy liberal solemnities of Spender's *Trial of a Judge* and the religious solemnities of *Murder In The Cathedral* look now essentially undramatic. The distinction made in *The Thirties* between parable-art and escape-art in the Auden/Isherwood plays treated them far too seriously. The authors were simply having fun, of an adolescent rather than a sophisticated Craig-Martin kind. When fun was abandoned for an attempt to write straightforward social drama in *On The Frontier* the result was dismally turgid. My belief that the two earlier plays 'were really a presage of something new', looking forward to Theatre Workshop's Brendan Behan plays, *Oh What A Lovely War* (the impact of which was much softened when it moved from East London to the West End) and the Littlewood version of *The Good Soldier Schweik* was similarly astray. This was not fully apparent, to me at least, until Brecht was generally available on the English stage. The comedy in *The Good Woman of Szechuan, Puntila* and other plays is savage, that of British would-be Brechtians flippant or inept. Verse drama in English faded away into the rhetoric of Christopher Fry and the drawing-room tragedies of late Eliot.

The attempt by the Thirties poets to write verse drama can be seen as a gallant but misguided move in the direction of producing work for a mass audience without sacrificing anything of group together-ness. An unperformed, and very likely unplayable, drama Roy Fuller and I collaborated on in the late Thirties had at least the negative merits of an awareness that social drama must be serious, that satire or irony should be used rather than flippant comedy, and that the model should be Ibsenic prose rather than Gilbert and Sullivan verse. It was, however, the drama in which the writers failed rather than the poetry, and lack of dramatic skill and seriousness doesn't affect the grandeur of Auden's choruses, or even the conversational verse spoken by Mr and Mrs A in *The Ascent of F.6.*

In literature the Thirties was essentially a poetic decade, and more than that Àuden's decade. I suppose many who come to the period freshly will question the assumption taken for granted by most of his contemporaries, that Auden was the most important English poet of the century. There was, to be sure, an opposition case being made even during the Thirties. At the time it did no more than rumble underground, but more recently it has been openly made, most clearly perhaps in *The 1930s: A Challenge To Orthodoxy.* In this collection of essays Edgell Rickword said that Auden, although 'aware of the decadence of bourgeois society', didn't really understand the alternative, and another contributor while granting Auden 'undeniable' talent, suggested that to call Auden and his friends the only interesting writers around was to support an orthodoxy 'rubbish-founded and a-litter with lies'. Twenty pages of poems by Randall Swingler and eighty pages of poetry and drama by Montagu Slater were printed as part of the 'challenge to orthodoxy'. But Swingler was not alien to the assumed 'orthodoxy' represented by the Auden group, simply a less talented writer in the same kind, and Slater's gifts were for prose drama, and opera in which verse played a lesser part.

A different kind of challenge to this imagined Thirties orthodoxy is offered by Cunningham, based not on weaknesses in Auden's poetry but in his character. He was characteristic, Cunningham says, of 'the 30s Peter Pan author in whom adulthood and childhood are curiously merged', a 'scoutmaster-schoolmaster writer...oddly indistinguishable from the schoolboys they should already have stopped being'. This schoolmaster-poet was as 'inhumanly casual about violence' as a schoolboy, until he actually glimpsed it in Spain. Cunningham is not very keen on the genuinely tough intellectuals who went to Spain, like John Cornford who as a friend said would as soon kick an opponent as anything else, but at least Cornford gets awards for honesty. Cunningham's view of Auden is that his bold poetic talk didn't match up to his timid or cowardly actions, and that this must affect our regard for the poetry.

It is true that reminiscences of Auden, and Humphrey Carpenter's biography, have destroyed the myth of him as a figure expressing the wisdom of his generation. Writing at the end of the Fifties I still more or less adhered to this illusion, even though a reference is made to his changes of stance and hesitations. It is disconcerting, no doubt about it, to find that 'Letter to a Wound' in *The Orators* had a physical origin in an unhealed anal fissure, and to learn that the views advanced with such apparent confidence were often no more than experimental expositions of an attitude, something more than gestures but less than expressions of deep or permanent feeling. Ideas about such matters as the psychological origins of illness, the liar's quinsy 'and the distortions of ingrown virginity', were picked up by a wide-ranging but erratic mind, never altogether discarded but also never part of an organized system of belief. From 1940 onwards Auden often attended Holy Communion, and said private prayers, but emotional and physical backsliding from Christian doctrine was frequent. 'Never will his prick belong / To his world of right and wrong' says one of the notes to *New Year Letter*, an observation to which the poet adhered in belief and practice, ignoring its several obvious contradictions in relation to human behaviour. His beliefs remained the sum of his confusions, something accepted in the collection of Pascalian notes and reflections written at the end of the Thirties. Its title, 'The Prolific and the Devourer', came from Blake, and he called it 'a new Marriage of Heaven and Hell'. In it he disposed of the problem of the relation between politics and art with the simplicity that often marked his complex mind:

> Few of the artists who round about 1931 began to take up politics as an entirely new subject to write about, had the faintest idea of what they were letting themselves in for... If they are neither to ruin themselves nor harm the political causes in which they believe, they must stop and consider their position again. Their follies of the last eight years will provide them with plenty of food for thought.

No doubt it was himself Auden had primarily in mind. He went on to say that one's ears should be closed to the voice of the Tempter saying: 'Unless you take part in the class struggle you cannot become a major writer', and that the political history of the world would have remained unaltered if no poems had been written, pictures painted, music composed. Auden later condemned the implicit determinism of

'The Prolific and the Devourer', as he disowned or qualified almost every attitude he took up, but his view of the unimportance of politics to the artist remained unchanged, and was summarized in the remark: 'Poetry makes nothing happen'.

Auden then, was, not the powerful intellectual force eulogized by his Oxford contemporaries, and regarded with awe by those who knew him only through the demands and exhortations of the early poems, but a man of erratically brilliant mind, and as he wrote to Spender when excusing his use of drugs, a fundamentally weak character who needed the support of an elaborate system of habits that extended far beyond the use of 'uppers' and 'downers' to specific times and procedures for eating, sleeping and rising. He denied, much more emphatically than many of us knew at a time when 'The Prolific and the Devourer' had not been published, the beliefs and sentiments of his Thirties poems.

One could conduct a running argument with Auden's remarks just quoted, pointing out that it is merely denigratory to say that artists approached politics as a new sensation rather than from a belief in the necessity of what they were doing, and that only the crudest political theorists would have used that phrase about writing and the class struggle. But such details of dissent are unimportant. The point to be made is that Auden's defects of character and confusions of thought don't affect the power and beauty of the poems he wrote in the decade. If this is what political beliefs did for Auden's poetry, then one might say with a crudeness equal to his own, hurrah for political beliefs. Cunningham's attack is effective so far as it concerns some of Auden's personal qualities, but doesn't touch the poems. Indeed, typical of critics in his generation, he makes no attempt to judge their quality.

I should take this defence of poetry which had roots in a political stance beyond consideration of an individual poet, and say it was positively helpful to poets in the Thirties. Not to all poets, however. Political feeling gave to Day Lewis's work sometimes a hectoring, at other times a lyrical, tone gratingly forced and sentimental. Such gruesome examples of what politics did to, or for, other poets are to be found in *The Thirties*. The effects on proletarian or would-be pro-letarian writers is also suggested, and is much amplified in Cunning-ham's book – although that is not altogether his intention, some of his rare expressions of praise being reserved for prose writers like the miners Joe Corrie, B.L. Coombes and Sid Chaplin. Yet there seems to me no doubt that political feeling, distinct from adherence to a theory or a party, was beneficial to Spender's work during the period, and that the development of an undogmatic political humanism was the root of MacNeice's *Autumn Journal*, one of the rare poems dealing with topical material that looks better today than when it was written. For younger poets like Kenneth Allott, Roy Fuller, George Woodcock, Ruthven Todd, politics, treated in general and sometimes even mythical terms, offered an entrance to poetry that might otherwise have lapsed into sentimental or dully introverted writing. The Spanish conflict moved George Barker to one of his finest poems, 'Elegy on Spain', and it could even be maintained that Dylan Thomas might have been a better poet if he had been touched more often by the political impulse that prompted 'The hand that signed the paper felled a city'. Another line in Davie's poem, 'A neutral tone is nowadays preferred', is less damaging to Thirties pretensions than it looks at first glance. The dry neutral tone of the Fifties and the retreat into purely technical concerns of the Seventies produced a lot of neuter poetry, as the confessional voice of the Sixties was responsible for much dismal investigation of uninteresting souls. The social concerns of Thirties poets put them in contact with a world outside their own bodies and emotions. Of course a lot of them wrote badly, like poets in any period.

The prose writers benefited similarly. In *The Thirties* all prose fiction except that deriving from Kafkaesque symbolism was ignored, and it still seems to me that an approach moving outside the limits of realism produced the most interesting social fiction of the decade. (I should say that something like the reverse is true at the moment, and that the novel would benefit greatly if the 'magical' was dropped from 'magical realism'.) But I should have said something about other fiction inspired by a variety of moral and social concerns. The most successful Thirties prose was certainly that untouched by propaganda for a class, a party or a movement. Isherwood's Berlin stories, and *Mr Norris Changes Trains*, remain successful novels as well as interesting documents of the time because everything is implied, nothing stated, and Nazism remains a thundercloud that in the stories never breaks into a storm. Attempts at Zolaesque realism were much less successful, although Lewis Grassic Gibbon's *Scots Quair* trilogy was much praised. Cunningham, acknowledging the 'ungainly and blunt' nature of much proletarian fiction, still says it 'did reveal working-class life, did put working-class regions of Britain, the humble parts of cities and their ordinary denizens, very firmly on the twentieth-century novel's map'. None of these stories of working-class life, however, was nearly as convincing as James T. Farrell's *Studs Lonigan* trilogy, in part because they were concerned with misery and hardship in a way that turned individual cases into general statements. Some of Arthur Calder-Marshall's novels, including *Dead Centre* and *About Levy*, are more successful because of a less obvious emphasis on social concern and a more limited scope. Again, the deliberate search for popularity was damaging. One can be sure that the Left Book Club, with its fifty thousand members, would have found Isherwood's Berlin stories not whole-heartedly anti-Fascist enough for its members.

To sum up: the general view now that socio-political concerns had a disastrous effect on Thirties writing is wrong. On the contrary, it was a positive virtue in poets and novelists that they approached their work from a social, even a specifically political point of view. Those who played down to the lowest common denominator of a large Audience failed, both artistically, and because they were writing for an Audience that did not exist.

7

Orwell's Decade?

Orwell was given no more than a page in *The Thirties*, treatment that has seemed extraordinary to some young students who felt that the hopes, doubts and beliefs of the decade were expressed more clearly in prose than poetry, by Orwell rather than Auden. That was not how it seemed at the time, nor how it looks to me in retrospect. The fame of *Animal Farm* and *Nineteen Eighty-Four* has carried along with it the earlier books, but if Orwell had died in 1939 he would be remembered now only as an interesting maverick who wrote some not very successful novels, a lively account of a few hard weeks in Paris, a quirky book about the miners that was somehow combined with an attack on sandalled vegetarian Socialists, and another offering a heterodox view of the Spanish Civil War. If he had died before writing either of the later fictions, or any of the remarkable Forties essays, this last would have been his most likely claim to remembrance.

During the Thirties, then, few regarded Orwell seriously as writer or thinker, and his ideas and allegiances shifted throughout the decade. After his Spanish experience and the writing of *Homage to Catalonia*, he was convinced of the need to plan underground resistance in the coming struggle against Fascism, and wrote to an alarmed Herbert Read suggesting that those who 'opposed the coming war' should 'start organising for illegal anti-war activities'. The chances of Labour winning an election he assessed as nil, and in any case he regarded the Labour Party bosses as not very different from the Chamberlain Government. They would join the Government in using the pretext of war with Germany to enforce 'wage reductions, suppression of free speech, brutalities in the colonies, etc.', and therefore dissidents must oppose the Left as well as the Right. 'I doubt whether there is much hope of saving England from fascism of one kind or another, but clearly one must put up a fight', and if printing presses were installed 'in some discreet place', they would at least be ready for the crackdown on free speech he expected.

Orwell wrote this letter to Read in March 1939. It is an interesting period document, because what may now seem moonshine was then the basis for a desperate optimism Orwell shared with others. There were many on the left, myself included, who believed the Chamberlain Government favoured Fascism, and might be replaced by one determined to resist the further spread of German or Italian rule in Europe. The question of the peaceful or bloody nature of the overturn was something blinked at rather than seriously considered, and the assumption was made that the armed forces might join a rebellion against the pro-Fascist government, and would at least refuse to shoot their working-class comrades. Such illusions were based on a romantic view of events in Russia in 1917, and they were I suppose no sillier than the illusions nursed by French students and others in 1968. But this kind of Thirties thinking was a very temporary stopping point for Orwell. With the advent of war he immediately abandoned such dreams of victory through revolutionary defeatism (to use a phrase of the time), in favour of support for 'my country Right or Left', even, as he said, support of the Chamberlain Government.

It would be wrong to call this later figure the 'real' Orwell, since what we say at one time in our lives is as real as what we say at another. What is certain, though, is that Orwell's finest work, the most perceptive essays, the marvellous fable, and the flawed but memorable fantasy of a permanent Doomsday, sprang from a patriotic attitude which he managed to combine with egalitarian Socialism. But these were not beliefs he held in the Thirties. The Forties were Orwell's decade.

8

Waiting for Doomsday

A little, but not enough, is said in *The Thirties* about the feelings of guilt that oppressed the writers most closely involved with the Thirties movement. (I note parenthetically that they did not touch Anthony Powell or Evelyn Waugh, whose opposition to the ideas and intentions of the movement was total.) It was the guilt expressed by Kafka that drew us to him, but unlike Kafka's central characters we were able to find many reasons for feeling guilty, from the time we woke in the morning to the resting of our uneasy heads on the pillow at night.

There were such obvious reasons as not going to fight in Spain or not joining either the Labour or Communist Parties, but others were more recondite. Many of those who did join a political party flinched from the boredom of ward or area meetings, the tedium of selling papers at street corners or putting leaflets in envelopes, but suffered pangs of guilt about their backsliding. And then most of us had to earn a living, and take a job that directly or indirectly supported the capitalist system we opposed. Was it right to work in an advertising agency or a newspaper office, when the copy or the news stories we wrote often contradicted our basic beliefs? There were further guilt feelings about taking an office job rather than doing manual work, but along with recognition of our incapacity to do the job of a bricklayer or miner went the knowledge that they too were part of the capitalist system. A different, more personal burden of guilt was involved in parent-child relationships. The habits and beliefs of our parents seemed to us ridiculous, and it was a duty to rebel against them, but the demands of affection meant that the rebellion was often limited to flouting of the parents' way of life rather than the complete severance of parental ties that the ideas of the Promethean movement suggested. And even the flouting involved guilt, first about behaving badly, and then about acting with such unPromethean feebleness by not cutting the parental knot.

Social guilt was involved also, when one read about the advance of Fascism throughout Europe, and recognized that nothing but organized military resistance was likely to stop it – nothing, that is, except those peaceful or violent revolutions that became increasingly distant mirages as the decade advanced. Some clung to the hope of an effective Popular Front including the Soviet Union, others adhered to a dream of effective pacifism, but for the two years before September 1939 we were really all waiting for a Doomsday we dreaded, yet longed for because it would finally absolve us from guilt.

To anybody under forty today such feelings will certainly seem absurd, and probably also unintelligible. We lived under the threat of domination by German Fascism, but in the 1990s the menaces are multifold. The end of civilized life on the planet by nuclear war is obviously the greatest, but its slower destruction by changes in the ozone layer seems equally likely, and a vast increase in violence looks certain as the norm of behaviour is changed through the widespread use of drugs. Yet, a man or woman of the Nineties might say, we remain cheerful in the face of this dismal prospect, and feel none of the guilt symptoms you are talking about. They might go on to point out that the War, after all, was won, Fascism was destroyed and Communist dictatorships are going the same way, so that Europe is becoming a set of nation states that may well have a beneficial unity and common aims. It's hard to see – these inhabitants of the Nineties might say – why you were so worried. Indeed, without using terms like lily-livered, isn't it a fact that you just weren't tough enough to live in the real world? How did one of the Thirties poets put it? 'How shall we live except as plants or fays / Who cannot take ten deep breaths in any crowd?'.

I should admit there was justice in such chiding. There is a fatalistic and lachrymose note in some writing, especially of the late Thirties, that makes it seem lacking in energy and written to a preconceived formula, like some of the laments of the Shropshire Lad, or most of Dowson's dirges for an imaginary lost happiness. And obviously there is something ridiculous about the way we fed on guilt, worrying at it like a dog with a bone that doesn't provide much nutriment but is still enjoyable to gnaw. Yet there is something more to be said. It was not only or principally self-pity that powered the best writing of the Thirties, but true concern for a civilization in its broad aspects gentle and rational, confronted by a barbarism passionate and vicious. Even the self-deception of the Pragmatists and some of the Artists about the virtues of Stalin's Soviet Union seems comprehensible when one considers the awful nature of Hitler's Germany.

(Although it should be added that the years since *The Thirties* was published have revealed how shameful was the behaviour of those who saw the betrayals in Spain and Moscow at first-hand, and still praised jovial Uncle Joe.) It is true also that after Munich we sensed the immediacy of Doomsday, where our Nineties counterparts cannot feel nuclear annihilation as anything but a nebulous threat. In part this is because the possibility of atomic or nuclear destruction has existed now for almost half a century, in part because total extinction is something much harder to imagine than total slavery. And the young have been aware of the possibility of total destruction since they were children, and know it cannot be wished away. There was a possibility, for perhaps two decades after Hiroshima when nuclear bombing capacity was confined to very few nations, that a slow mutual disarmament might take place. There was some point then in protest marches. But those days are long gone, and protest marches in Europe or the United States are pointless now that civilization depends for its continued existence on the good sense and goodwill of such dubious figures as the rulers of Israel, Algeria, and Iraq.

Nor can we with any decency talk now about a Western civilization in its broad aspects gentle and rational. Terrible things have been done, or consented to, in the past thirty years by governments that would consider themselves civilized, ranging from the use of lethal gases and consent to the torture of prisoners to such comparatively mild forms of oppression as treating national citizens of another belief or colour as inferiors. Television has played a large part in hardening our hearts to suffering. By revealing in pictures mass murder, deliberate starvation and individual acts of cruelty, it has inured us to them, so that we regard as inevitable actions that half a century ago would have caused a storm of protest. The acceptance of cruelty has seeped into our private lives, running alongside the demands for ever-increasing personal freedom that mark particularly the world's more prosperous countries.

Young men and women are more content with the world they live in than we were in the Thirties, and the prospect of Doomsday does not consciously affect their minds, although it may unconsciously order their actions. Yet they are basically less optimistic than we were half a century ago, for they have abandoned hope of changing in any basic way the nuclear-threatened world they live in. Those who waited for Doomsday in the Thirties were also waiting for Lefty. They were optimistic not only about improving the material conditions of most people by changes in society, but also about changing the essential nature of human beings. It goes against the grain, when considering the horrors perpetrated in the last half-century by many who would consider themselves good citizens, to admit that our optimism in the Thirties was mistaken.

9

Kermode on the Thirties

At the moment of writing, the beginning of the Nineties, the ideas and art of the Thirties have a bad press. Much the most generous recent assessment of them has been that made by Frank Kermode, in the Clarendon lectures later put between covers as the first part of *History and Value*. At least the Thirties writers saw the need to cross frontiers, he says; some died in the attempt, and although others retreated, their behaviour was not ignominious. The things they attempted were 'valuable to us, fifty years on'.

Professor Kermode seems too young (b.1919) to have been part of the Thirties (though if we remind ourselves of Gavin Ewart publishing poems in his mid-teens and David Gascoyne's novel appearing when he was seventeen, we realize that he might have been), but old enough to have been strongly aware of them. In that sense he is an ideal commentator, approaching things done and said with a sympathy remote from Cunningham, or even from Stephen Spender's retrospective view. Perhaps there are times when Kermode is almost too sympathetic, willing for the sake of making a point to investigate patiently writing or ideas that seem to call for instant dismissal. Academic caution blends with detached kindness to produce a tone so muted that it is not always certain whether irony can be discerned through the muffler, as when he says in relation to a *Left Review* competition that 'the intention was to open Literature, as the middle class understood the concept, to qualified aspirants from the working class – in short, to give that class access to what was known to be truly valuable'. Obviously ironic, one may think, but the treatment of this and similar approaches to an imagined proletarian literature is done with a perfectly straight face. And there are times when one wishes the kindness were a little more detached, as when he awards good conscience medals to those who joined the Party or fellow-travelled, on the ground that 'they were not climbing on to a bandwaggon' because 'even in the days of its greatest pre-war success... the Party had only a few thousand members'. What Party membership or fellow-travelling

gave, however, was membership of an élite who really *knew* what was
going on, unlike the general public who, as Auden put it, had 'no
notion / Of what's behind the scenes. / They vote at times with some
emotion / But don't know what it means.' Party members and fellow-
travellers read the gossip and fiction purveyed in Claud Cockburn's
news sheet *The Week*, and were happy in their superior knowledge of
the international situation.

These are minor matters. A more important qualification made by
Kermode to the ideas advanced in this postscript is the link he suggests
between the homosexuality of several Thirties writers and their political radicalism. Apparently quoting Lord Annan, Kermode says that
the inter-war period was 'the highwater mark of gentlemanly homosexuality' (a wonderfully ambiguous word, that 'gentlemanly'), and
suggests that middle-class homosexuals were searching for the Ideal
Friend, or the Other. They were also aware, he suggests, of their
emotional and practical alienation from the working class with whom
they longed to be one, and looked for the Ideal Friend in an attractive
working-class body, thus becoming in the most literal sense one with
the workers. 'Such is pastoral when it is about the possibility of love
between classes.'

This seems much too high-flown. A lot of middle-class interest in
working-class youths was little more than the equivalent of sexual
slumming, a Thirties variation on Wilde's romantic illusion that when
he took young working-class prostitutes to hotels he was feasting with
panthers. I should agree with a scurrilous Thirties rhyme about one
poet, that he 'confuses the working classes / With their arses'. Kermode illustrates his argument for this sort of pastoral by reference to
Edward Upward's trilogy *The Spiral Ascent* and Edmund Wilson's
'The Girl With The Golden Hair', which both deal with love affairs
between intellectuals and working-class girls, who are seen as giving
their lovers 'that life of the people which had before been but prices
and wages' in Wilson's case, and in Upward's a kind of sanctification
of the working-class as a whole, achieved by well-born Alan Sebrill
through the wretched nature of the maisonette in which he will settle
down to live with the physically unattractive girl he marries. ('Oh
Elsie, you are so ugly', he wails.) Kermode sees the absurdity of Alan's
attitude, but seems to feel that the merit of the attempt to cross the
class barrier outweighs the sanctimoniousness of Wilson's narrator
and the self-conscious superiority of Alan Sebrill. He is customarily so
poker-faced in comment that positive opinions about individual works

are rarely offered, but he does call Upward's trilogy (set in the Thirties, although published long afterwards) remarkable, and expresses admiration for its 'refined structures and transformations'. Those like me who found the trilogy deadly dull, and marked by an astonishing imperceptiveness of the way people talk – after calling Elsie ugly, Alan asks her to forget his 'unforgivable outburst' – can only dissent.

It is a prime merit of Kermode's lectures, transcending argument about the quality of Upward's work, that they return constantly to the matter of class consciousness and class alienation, illuminating general points with detailed examination of particular works like *Dead Centre*, and the posthumously-published novel *We Live*, by the Welsh miner Lewis Jones. This was a main theme of the decade, glanced at in *The Thirties* in relation to the gap between homosexual Oxford- or Cambridge-educated poets and heterosexual writers who had not attended even a red-brick University, but not dealt with in anything like such attentive detail. A distinction is made between the pangs of conscience felt by every new generation of do-gooders for the past two centuries, and what is said to be the unique feeling among writers in the Thirties 'about inequality and the absence of respect and affection between classes', which led not just to do-goodism but to the belief that poverty and class hatred could be eliminated only through 'vast historical change, revolution and war'. This perception, going to the heart of what was seen as an inevitable, permanent alienation between the intellectual and the worker in Western society, is rightly said to be a different feeling from any experienced by such sympathizers as Morris, Ruskin or Shaw. Again, a little of this was said in *The Thirties*, but it is put more clearly and sympathetically in these lectures. I suppose one should add that the feeling, and the need for it, would not be understood by young intellectuals in the Nineties who are not concerned with gaps between classes, but with racism, sexism, élitism.

In the Thirties, however, we felt as guilty about class as many are today about race or sex. We agreed with Auden that 'You can't, at least in this world, change your class', and perhaps those least bothered by that accepted fact were members of the lower-middle-class like me, who had intellectual aspirations but shared a good many working-class assumptions and habits. Kermode seems to come from a roughly similar background, except that he was brought up in the Isle of Man and not in South London, but he shows what seem to me some failures of understanding in this matter of class, interesting

particularly because of his sympathetic approach. His stance is at
times a little like that of working-class figures in the Thirties, who
were very keen to sniff out and attack condescension. MacNeice is
mildly rebuked for saying that Birmingham is a sprawling inkblot
and living on the city's genteel south side, Barker for calling Bour-
nemouth's public gardens 'marvellous' when (Kermode says) he
really means 'what ordinary people ignorantly think marvellous', a
plurality of writers for regarding cinemas as a pathetic solace for the
poor. (But weren't they very generally regarded as dream factories
from the Twenties onwards?) The climax of his attack on what he
sees as intellectual condescension to the poor comes through analysis
of some lines by Kenneth Allott describing

> The greengrocer's cart, the haggling to save a halfpenny
> On the boiled orange or the Argus-eyed potato;
> The fecund red-elbowed women with their baskets,
>   And their humourless menfolk.
>
> These will never hold aces or travel farther
> Than a tram will take them. And their summum bonum
> The threepenny double which comes up by a head,
>   Unlimited bitter.

The long poem, 'Men Walk Upright', is granted indignation and
compassion (it is a meditation, written with Allott's almost unfalter-
ing felicity of phrase, on the virtues of accepting the world rather
than trying to change it), but Kermode comments that it 'certainly
makes the poor keep their distance', condemns the quoted lines for
a variety of condescensions, is baffled by the boiled orange, and ends
with his own touch of condescension by saying that 'to see [the
poem's] value requires a patient effort of historical understanding'.
It may need some historical understanding, or at least some knowledge of greengrocers' fiddles in the past, to understand the boiled
orange, which gets another whimsical reference or two. The phrase
refers to a common working-class belief that some greengrocers boiled
oranges so that they swelled up in size, and the flavourless but hefty
result appeared to be good value. The boiled orange mystery aside,
the quoted lines seem to me to show a detached sympathy for those
who will never hold aces and won't often see court cards, although
certainly the detachment is as apparent as the sympathy. This is not

a matter of saying that one view of Allott's lines, or of the approach to working-class feelings in Upward's trilogy, is 'correct' or the reverse. The point is that even an effort of understanding as genuine as Kermode's is necessarily made from an attitude different from that of a true Thirties denizen.

10

Deconstructing Value Judgements

In the course of his Clarendon lectures, and the Northcliffe lectures that followed, Kermode also had a good deal to say about the question of literary values. His pronouncements typically blend boldness and caution, acknowledging that in 'unofficial conversation' we are all prepared to distinguish sound from rotten among creative works, but become delphic when confronted with the problem of saying why ' "our" kind of writing has most "merit" and "aesthetic value".' It is true that this question is finally unanswerable, in the sense that there is no way of *proving* that Lewis Jones's *We Live*, the novel Kermode happened to have under consideration, is not the equal of *Middlemarch* or *Bleak House*, any more than I was able to answer satisfactorily the crime writer who asked me why his work was not comparable with Shakespeare's, since they were equally concerned with crime and violence, the difference between verse and prose seeming to him a minor one. William Gerhardi's answer to this problem of value judgement was to say simply 'I know and you don't know', but although that was a solution for him it leaves the rest of us where we were, every man or woman his or her own Gerhardi.

The Thirties view that all creative work should be seen first in relation to the social conditions and morality that produced it was stated at the beginning of this postscript. It should not, however, be taken to mean that the literary content of literature, the painterly content of painting, can be taken as secondary elements, nor that the socially progressive or reactionary attitude of a writer or painter can determine the value of their work. In the end this too must be a matter of individual judgement, whether the subject is Dostoevsky or Sholokhov, a Wyndham Lewis or a Lewis Jones. I can see that if the judgement is finally so purely individual, it may be reasonable to ask the point of worrying about particular social conditions and morality. The reply would be that it does in practice make a difference to what we think of a creative work if we approach it first as an object in society. Some works, like religious paintings of the centuries before the Renaissance, are so remote in their content for those belonging to our secular culture that, for the secular, they can be appreciated only on a painterly level. Others have an immediate appeal because they anticipate our own ways of thinking about things and looking at them. A social approach may illuminate, but what must be decisive in the end is the exposure of any work of the imagination to the sluice of hearing and seeing – which may mean that we are back with Gerhardi, but a Gerhardi whose reactions are controlled by something more than purely aesthetic feeling.

This reiteration of a Thirties stance must, I'm aware, look quite irrelevant to any Post-Modernist. About this Kermode has very good, clear and coherent things to say, not the least valuable being the fact that Post-Modernism can mean almost anything any proponent wants it to mean. 'Postmodernism...does not symbolise but signify, it is a presence and not the symbol of an absence.' Its origins lie in the destruction of philosophical abstract values during this century, in which A.J. Ayer's *Language, Truth and Logic* played such an important part. If words are mere counters, meaningless unless they have direct application to objects, there is no validity in attempting to corral words like Goodness, Truth and Beauty and attach meaning to them, as philosophers have traditionally done. The philosopher's job is rather to analyse words and relate them, not to an objective 'reality', for that has no existence, but to the ideas of reality in the mind of each individual. The purposes of philosophy are thus omnivalent yet totally subjective, reminiscent to the sciolist of Berkeleyan solipsism. The end result is the deconstruction of a non-existent objective 'reality' into its innumerable actual parts.

That last paragraph may I'm afraid seem like Modern Philosophy For Tiny Tots. I am not qualified to engage in argument about the philosophical concepts behind the words *structuralism* and *deconstruction*. My concern is only with the consequences when these concepts are extended to literature under the name of Post-Modernism, and then because of their philosophical origins treated as given truths. Argument is not possible with a Post-Modernist, any more than with a convinced Freudian, because any discussion with them will start with assumptions that to the outsider are expressions of faith. Any other starting point the Post-Modernist simply finds unacceptable. Thus, to say that a book is or may be a work of art seems to him meaningless. All books are texts for Post-Modernists, and each text has as many possible meanings as there are readers. When one reader says 'art' another may say 'tedium' and a third 'nonsense'. A response that the views of some readers are more valuable than those of others would be regarded as unprovable verbalism.

Much follows from this basic idea that a creative work is a text, susceptible to an infinite number of interpretations. One work is as interesting as another, and no touchstones of excellence can be admitted to exist. Cynthia Ozick puts it well, in the course of an examination of the decline of Eliot's reputation among the American young, so that (she tells us) he survives only as 'two or three pages in the anthologies, a fleeting assignment for high-school seniors and college freshmen'. The lack of interest in a culture referring back to the past marks, she says, a situation in which

> High art is dead. The passion for inheritance is dead. Tradition is equated with obscurantism. The wall that divided serious high culture from the popular arts is breached; anything can count as 'text'... Allusiveness is cross-cultural in an informational and contemporary way (from, say, beekeeping to film-making), rather than in the sense of connecting the present with the past. The relation of poets to history is that they can take it or leave it, and mostly they leave it, whether in prosody or in the ideas of the venerable.

She adds that 'not to incorporate into an educable mind the origins and unifying principles of one's own civilization strikes me as a kind of cultural autolobotomy.' Examples of that autolobotomy in progress can be seen in the praise for Warhol, and in current interpretations of Shakespeare. The examples given could be multiplied many times.

There is something so absolutely nonsensical about this extension of philosophical theory to literature that it is hard to understand why anybody takes it seriously. Kermode, remarking on Post-Modernist preference for the fragment over the whole, observes that twenty years ago, when he heard that syntactically ordered sentences were being called Fascist, he asked if it would be a good democratic idea to randomize the telephone book. A nice joke, but elsewhere he finds it necessary to indulge Post-Modernism by considering it seriously rather than venturing on outright condemnation, wrestling over two or three pages with the complexities involved in Terry Eagleton's attempts to force elements of Post-Modernism into Marxism. But at least he tackles the propositions of Post-Modernism head on rather than tacitly accepting them like some of his contemporaries, and points out that in practice Post-Modernists play the game of distinguishing sound from rotten as readily as those devoted to Gerhardiesque individualism. For the Post-Modernist the fragmentary is inevitably preferred to the ordered, but 'modern fragments in a poet you like are Modernist, in a poet you don't like merely modern'.

It would be wrong, however, to think that in relation to literature Post-Modernists are merely talking about fragments in relation to organized wholes. Structuralism and deconstruction, as applied to literature, provide the theoretical justification for the levelling process already shown at work in this postscript. Behind a movement that may appear at first glance wholly concerned with verbal abstraction a social force is at work, one driving insistently in the arts towards a grinding equalitarianism that would put novel, poem, film and play on the same level, and that has an outcome in the belief that Post-Modern attitudes can be useful in advancing social causes. Kermode quotes a forecast for future 'literary studies' in the United States which says that the 'dominant concern' of literary theory in the next few years will be using the work of the structuralist philosopher Jacques Derrida 'to gain insights into the culture of blacks and women'. Phrases about this prospect like 'challenging nexus' and 'exciting and insightful' lead on to the triumphant observation that 'such theoretical accounts of the cultural products of race and gender will help to understand the half-truths that white males have established as constituting American culture as a whole', followed by the promise or threat that 'literary theory is also full of disruptive and deeply political potential' waiting to be released.

If we try to assess Post-Modernism logically, it should have nothing to do with such directly social concerns as black or female culture, nor should it be worrying about 'American culture as a whole', since one strand of the movement emphasizes that culture as a whole does not exist. But Post-Modernists are not restricted by logic, and to serve their social purpose are quite ready to envisage a 'whole' American culture, even one composed of half-truths, so that it can be seen as a model to be destroyed in the service of the black and female cultures that will replace it. What began as philosophical speculation is being converted to practical use, and its purpose is not creation but destruction. There is no prospect in the near future of the 'cultural products of race and gender' replacing those established by 'white males' throughout the centuries, but if what Ozick calls 'serious high culture' can be brought down to the level of popular art, and the standards created by white males (some white females too) totally eroded, why then, the way may be clear for the acceptance of anything at all as art. It would be a world in which the Beatles are equal to Bach and Beethoven, Christie is one with Chaucer and Lichtenstein with Leonardo, and a good TV soap may be considered on the same terms as a Shakespeare play. Those critics who would agree with the drift of what I am saying, yet out of good nature, sympathy with minority groups, or fear of offending fashion, fail to point out the fraudulent nature of minimalist art today and the inferiority of almost all popular art when judged by any high standard – who refuse to invoke the very existence of standards by which to judge – are tacitly assisting the progress of Post-Modernism.

The problem addressed is not new, although it is not apparent in every period, and does not always take such a destructive form. It appeared in the Thirties in the form of an attempt to elevate the claims of work produced, particularly by proletarian writers but also by those of middle- or lower-middle-class origin, in the service of the proletariat. Such work was compared favourably to what was then called mandarin or ivory-tower literature. Kermode, with too much kindness, identifies that as a remarkable moment in literary history, 'an attempt to unify bourgeois intellect and proletarian culture'. He invokes an imaginary self-questioning Thirties figure asking how 'we' can know that 'our' kind of writing is more aesthetically valuable than Lewis Jones's raw novel about hard working-class lives, when 'we' believe that literature like everything else takes its values from the supremacy of one class over another. The argument, stated differently, was that of what may conveniently be called *Left Review* intellectuals in the Thirties, and is at the heart of what is said by recent revisionists who would deny the supremacy of Auden and his followers as writers. That *as writers* would be for the revisionists an inadmissible tag, for they would feel it divorced writing from society. To the rest of us in the Thirties – that is, to those who rejected the limitations of the *Left Review* credo that 'a writer's usefulness depends on his influence: that is to say, on the size and enthusiasm of his public' – the problem was less disturbing than Kermode seems to think. It was, rather, a matter of raising inferior proletarian culture to the level of bourgeois culture. Those who believed proletarian literature could flourish in a bourgeois society were attempting, more diffidently, with less sophistication and much less success, the levelling process now taking place under the anti-intellectual intellectual cloak of deconstructionist theory.

Does all or some of this postscript sound hostile to blacks, feminists, homosexuals? That is not intended, although many of the attitudes taken up by those who claim to speak for these groups seem to me likely to defeat the ends they profess. Homosexuals should be regarded on terms of social equality with heterosexuals, but this will not be encouraged by the establishment of bars, clubs and magazines which suggest that they make up an entirely separate section of society; women should work on terms of equality with men, but it is foolish to pretend that equality in other matters can ever be exact since the physical and emotional make-up of the sexes is different; and although it is natural to sympathize with those who, in Britain and elsewhere, suffer in white societies because they have a different skin colour, nobody will benefit by the pretence that their literature and art should replace those of the white societies in which they live.

Such rash candour seems necessary, although the remarks are a little to the side of the essential points I have been making about differences between the Thirties and the Nineties. The mistakes made in the Thirties through trying to blend high art and idealistic politics were many, but at least most of us made no concessions to art in the name of society. Our brows remained high (I read the other day that the term *highbrow culture* is now certainly out of fashion), and whatever sacrifices we were prepared for in the service of a better society, value judgements in literature were not among them.

The most dismaying aspect of what looks to lie ahead in the Nineties is that many would-be creators and practising critics seem prepared to enter happily enough a world of art in which, to use Wyndham Lewis's phrase, nothing is preferred to something, and that in literature those who speak in the name of deconstruction wish to abandon all value judgements, often in the service of what they regard as an ignored black or feminist culture. Yet value judgements are the life of art, and the values of the past germinate the art of any interesting future, for it is the actualities of the past that all art springs from, even art that dissents violently from them in some particulars. After a nuclear disaster, art, except in its most elementary form, would cease to exist. To quote Lewis again: 'Infantile extreme sensationalism is the curse of the pundit. What every artist should try to prevent is the car, in which is our civilized life, plunging over the side of the precipice – the exhibitionist extremist promoter driving the whole bag of tricks into a nihilistic nothingness or zero.' Those words were written in the early Fifties. They sound prophetic today.